Morning Drum

John Christie, 1940

Morning Drum

by
John Christie

BACSA
PUTNEY, LONDON
1983

Published by the British Association
for Cemeteries in South Asia.
Secretary: Theon Wilkinson,
76½ Chartfield Avenue,
London SW 15

ISBN 0 907799 04 3

Printed by The Chameleon Press
5-25 Burr Road, Wandsworth, London SW 18 4SG

Contents

And he, that points the Centonell his roome,
Doth license him depart at sound of morning droome.

Spenser: The Faerie Queene
(Bk 1 canto IX.XLI)

For Elizabeth

Foreword

This is the third of a series of books written by a BASCA member, published by BASCA, for BASCA members with a wider public in mind.

The author of this book, W.H.J. Christie, CSI, CIE, OBE, joined the Indian Civil Service in 1928 and served first in Bengal (Mymensingh, Asansol, Calcutta and the Chittagong Hill Tracts), then in New Delhi with Government of India departments and on the staff of three viceroys including Mountbatten. After Independence in 1947 he stayed on for twelve years in business capacities in New Delhi and Kanpur. This ground is well covered in the main chapters of the book and there is also a revealing early section on childhood, schooldays and university going into the making of a member of the ICS. The book speaks for itself and needs no further introduction except to provide the author with an opportunity to express acknowledgements due.

****

'The first of these, in the case of 'Morning Drum' is to the Editor of Blackwood's Magazine for his encouragement and his ready consent to my reproducing material which I had contributed to 'Maga' at intervals before it ceased publication. I am grateful, too, to my neighbour, Mrs Alice Scadden, who patiently reduced a jungle of ill-typed pages and corrections into a presentable script, and to my daughter, Mrs Valentine Parry, for her drawing of a drummer boy. Finally, I wish to light a small candle to Dr. E.C. Brewer, in the pages of whose Dictionary of Phrase and Fable I found support, in correspondence between East Africa and Edinburgh for my contention that the 'Brocken Spectre' (see at the end of Chapter 3 within), although an illusion, really existed. Blackwoods had changed it to 'Brocken Spectrum' in order to remove a stumbling block for unwary readers of their magazine. Dr. Brewer, however, records:
>"Spectre of Brocken. An optical illusion, first observed on the Brocken (the highest peak of the Hartz range in Saxony), in which shadows of the spectators, greatly magnified, are projected on the mists about the summit of the mountain opposite. In one of De Quincey's opium dreams there is a powerful description of the Brocken Spectre"

John Christie, 1983

'The drummer boy' by Mrs. Valentine Parry

1

The Drummer

As soon as the first sun-ray stabbed through the reed curtain of the tent, I was out of bed, pulled on my shirt and trousers, thrust my feet into sandals and was on my way to the river bank, before the voice of authority could call me back. The air was crisp as I ran through the tamarisk bushes, avoiding the melon pits. The sunlit mist, just lifting off the water, was shoulder high, and my warm breath added to its volume.

The life of a camp-follower was good: I wished it could go on forever. Last year I had wanted to join the gypsies, whose bare feet could, without reproof, scuffle the soft dust of the roadside as they went their way in laughing, singing parties, dark men with earrings and many-coloured headcloths, the women's skirts swinging and brass anklets jingling; and among them was a boy who had all that my own heart could then desire, for round his neck was slung a long drum from which he drew a throbbing melody with the fingers of one hand, while with the other he led a performing bear.

But this winter I had put away childish things. I was part of an army now, which, with my entire approval, left its stifling barracks for four months of the year, and moved about the countryside under canvas, not restlessly like the gypsies, but slowly and deliberately, stretching its limbs in peaceful exercise. Camp meant change of scene, adventure, new companionships, combined with the security of home; in fact it had most of the attributes of my idea of heaven. I had forgotten the gypsies: all that remained for me of last year's encounter with them was an irresistible longing to play the drum.

Of all that camp life had to offer, it was companionship I was seeking now. Hira Lal was waiting by the stone slabs where the washermen were beating out clothes. He was nearly a year older than me and therefore entitled to respect, which is a more compelling relationship than obedience.

"They have killed a goat in the butchers' lines, and cut it open," he said. "It is hanging by its feet from a tree and bleeding. Come and see." I was not squeamish but such gory sights were not new to me.

"No, let's go and see the new fish traps you have made," I said. "Are they as good as Lakshman's traps?" Lakshman was Hira Lal's elder brother. He had hopes of promotion to be a side-drummer in the regimental band, and was a hero to both of us; he could do no wrong.

Hira Lal turned without a word and led the way down to the water's edge. There we bent over three ingenious contraptions of basket-work, woven with delicate slivers of split bamboo, partly submerged under the low bank and facing downstream in the slowly moving current. Hira Lal felt under the water and brought a tray to the surface. There was a flash of half a dozen leaping, silvery fingerlings.

"Well , my traps have caught fish" he said. "Lakshman's are over there," pointing upstream. Tacitly we agreed not to risk spoiling the sweet taste of success by comparison.

"How will you eat them?" I asked. "With rice, and curry?"

"Rice!" he said indignantly. "Do you take me for a Bengali? No, with wheat flour, ground in our hand-mill and made into chupattis, like this." He took a ball of wet clay and patted it rapidly between his hands until it was as flat as a pan-cake. "Then my mother will bake it on the iron. She will cook the fish in mustard oil, with chillies and tamarind and that yellow stuff, haldi, and I will pick them up, one by one, with pieces of chupatti to put in my mouth." He smacked his lips and slapped his stomach.

My own inner emptiness began to ache. Breakfast was still some way off. It must wait for my father to finish his morning round of inspections. I changed the subject.

"Has Lakshman got his drummer's badge yet?"

"Yesterday: and now he is so proud he will not speak to me. But before he became proud he told me something which concerns you. It is secret. I must not tell you."

He could not keep a secret. If I was patient, all would be revealed. "You may guess" he said. "If you guess right, I will not have told you."

I was gnawed by curiosity, but said nothing. We walked in silence some way towards the transport lines. The mules were being fed, and those that had not had their ration yet were complaining loudly of the injustice. Hira Lal was shouting above the din:

"It is a pity you did not come and look at that goat: then you might have guessed." I shouted back: "How can it have anything to do with me and with a dead goat that I have not seen?"

Suddenly the mules were silent, and another sound, more distant, could now be heard. It was a sound which never failed to excite me. The regimental band was practising: the roll of the side-drums, in quick-step two-four time, made my skin tingle, while the measured thud of the big drum was not so much a sound as a deep emotion in the pit of my stomach.

"Listen! Now can you guess?"

Now I knew, but I would not admit it.

"What do they make with goat-skins, blockhead?"

"They make water-carriers' pouches - and bladders to swim upon" I said, being dense on purpose.

"Drums, drums!" he shouted. "Lakshman is making a drum for you, and he will use the skin of that goat."

I was determined not to believe him. The jealousy of heaven must be averted.

"It cannot be. How can a caste Hindu handle a goatskin?"

"Why not? When the butcher and currier have finished with it, it will not be an animal skin, but a drum skin. And if you find some brown hairs sticking to it, you will know it is that very goat."

During the next few days the regiment was moving camp. Everyone was busy, and I heard no more about the drum. Then, one morning in new surroundings, outside my tent flap - there it was. My first instinct was one of fear, lest it should disappear before my eyes. Then joy and surprise. I had not dreamt of such a drum as this: the most I had hoped for - if Hira Lal had not made up the whole story - was that Lakshman might make me a gypsy drum, which is played with the hands at both ends. This was a far more glorious thing. It was a military side-drum, reduced to scale, the rims painted with the regimental colours of green and yellow in wavy lines, and shining brass between them, brass screws, real gut for snares, and a pipe-clayed, plaited lanyard underneath, to swing proudly as the drummer marched. A pair of black drumsticks and a broad leather shoulder-sling with a brass hook completed the outfit. It must have been the combined product of Lakshman and several other craftsmen. When I walked all round it, and could bear to examine it more closely, I found at the edge of the underskin a small patch of brown hair, which proclaimed its origin.

Then I put on the full regalia, and marched towards the sound of the distant drums. I did not approach too near, but joined the small crowd of camp children who, at a respectful distance, were a regular audience at the band practices. Among them I was able to show off, even venturing an inexpert roll or two when the drums were beating and the bugles blowing loud enough to drown my contribution.

The parade was dismissed. On the way back to camp Lakshman overtook me and gave me a greeting. I could find no

voice to utter my thanks, which lay too deep for words, but he
must have read them in my face.

"The Subedar has seen you with your drum" he said. "He
needs a recruit, and would like you to join our parade, if you
wish. But you should also practice by yourself. I will show
you. See, to strengthen the wrists take the drumsticks by the
heads pointing inwards, in one hand at a time, and swing them to
and fro. Then the roll - tap, tap, slowly at first, then faster
and faster, until you feel the sticks are rolling by themselves
thus - " He took the sticks from me and demonstrated with
enviable ease and skill. "Some day I will teach you the broken
roll; that is more difficult."

The Band Subedar was the father of Lakshman and Hira Lal.
He was a veteran with grizzled mustachios and a row of campaign
medals. He could play every instrument of martial music, even
the bagpipes, it was said, learnt on the North-West Frontier
from a Pipe-Major of the Black Watch.

When I ventured out with my drum next morning, the Band was
already on parade, standing in a circle.

"Do I see the recruit?" said the Subedar. "Come, stand
next to Lakshman. Why are you late?"

"My ayah made me change my shoes" I said.

"Ah, the tyranny of women in the camp!"
We practised stirring marches in two-four and six-eight time,
bugles and drums alternating in the lead. I watched, and
followed, as closely as I could, Lakshman's manoeuvres with his
drumsticks as he raised and lowered and clicked them in front of
his face; but I joined in the roll only at his signal, when all
the drums were beating in unison.

Suddenly there was silence. "Band - atten-shun!" said the
Subedar.

"Stand at ease" said a familiar voice. The Officer-of-
the-Day was on his rounds. He had a word or two with most of
the bandsmen as he walked round with the Subedar. I swallowed
hard as he approached me. He stood in front of me and looked up
and down. There was no word, nor flicker of recognition. As he
passed on to the next man - "I see you have a new recruit,
Subedar sahib" said my father.
"Yes, sir. He seemed keen, and brought his own drum. I am
giving him a trial."

"Is he obedient and punctual?"

"He is as punctual as is possible for a family man. He
tells me there are sometimes domestic obligations."

"Well, teach him to hold his head up, and look like a
soldier - like this young man, for instance" - he pointed to
Lakshman. "There's a good model for a recruit."
I saw the Subedar's moustaches twitch, and it seemed that his

chest expanded an inch or so.

At breakfast my mother said "The Band were very noisy this morning. Couldn't you get them to practise a little further away?"

"Bear with them, my dear," said my father. "I am told they have recruited a promising new drummer. Some increase of volume must be expected."

I caught his eye, and I am sure I saw one eyelid droop.

2
Salad Days

Some years later, in a different world (it seemed) a bugle sounded and another drum began to beat. Without haste, carbines at the trail, a small body of troops fell in on the level space that served as their parade ground. A word of command, and they moved off in fours across the open plain.

No advance guard, no flank guards – elementary precautions neglected, one would have thought – but almost as far as the eye could see, almost; but through the haze ahead, as they advanced, the outline of an escarpment began to take shape, at the foot of which they must pass. The slopes were covered with low scrub which, in shape and colour, might have been lavender on a sloping bank in Sussex.

Was there a stirring behind those bushes? Suddenly aware of the danger Captain Loseby, in charge of the party, barked an order. Again the bugle spoke. With practised ease and precision the troops formed square. Not a moment too soon, for simultaneously the air was rent with the war cries of a Zulu impi charging down the incline, and with the rattle of musketry.

The whites of the enemy's eyes were near enough for the marksmanship of the British soldier to take deadly effect. Prone and still, or contorted in agony under the muzzles of the carbines, within three minutes every Zulu warrior had bitten the dust.

That was in the early summer of 1914. The detachment was part ot the 2nd Home Counties Brigade, Royal Field Artillery; but artillery in name only. They had been trained to an infantry role, and not many of them had seen a field gun in their lives. They were very young soldiers indeed. Apart from the officer, their average age could not have been more than eleven years, for they were the cadet corps of a preparatory school, and their battle ground the playing field of St. Cyprian's, Eastbourne.

I was among the Zulus on that day, but I survived to be promoted to kneel in the square itself, and can therefore trace my lineal descent, in terms of military training, directly to the fields of Quatre Bras and Waterloo.

A roll-call of the soldiers and of the fallen savages, restored to life, might have included some interesting names. There, or in later engagements, would have been Bombardier Eric Blair (one day to be George Orwell) and Gunner Cyril Connolly; there, too, would have been Cecil Beaton - unless he had been excused parade to design dresses or paint scenery for the school play. Robert Foote, later to win the Victoria Cross and become an Armoured Corps general, was certainly present; and Seymour de Lotbiniere, a future pioneer of broadcasting, who had been nicknamed Lobengula by Mr Ellis, the maths master, must surely have been brandishing his assegai with the Zulus on that day. Henry Longhurst, I rather think, came later, or was of too tender an age even for mock warfare - he might have been caddying for our golf-addicted headmaster at the time of the battle.

How did I come to be in this distinguished company? My Indian background may have had something to do with it. There had been a tradition of Indian service on both the Scottish and Irish sides of my family. My father, in 1913, was a junior captain in the Indian Army. Three generations before him in the direct line, and numerous uncles and great-uncles, Christies and Humfreys, had soldiered in India. Old Tom Christie, who started the tradition, and rates a column in the Dictionary of National Biography, had been a surgeon in the Honourable East India Company's army, before Arthur Wellesley had won his spurs as a Sepoy General. He was a friend, and may have been a pupil of Edward Jenner, for he introduced vaccination into Ceylon. No doubt he vaccinated Mr Samuel Tolfrey, the Auditor-General in Colombo; at any rate he married his daughter.

Samuel Tolfrey had practised law in Calcutta as a young man, in the days of Warren Hastings, He had been one of Sir Philip Francis' attorneys in a cause célèbre, after the putative author of the Letters of Junius had been caught climbing up a ladder into a lady's bedroom while her husband was out to dinner. Samuel Tolfrey, according to an 18th century Calcutta scandal sheet, later became involved himself with the lady in question, but she aimed higher than a young attorney and finished up in Paris as Princesse de Talleyrand

This has little enough to do with St. Cyprian's or with me at the age of seven, but it may explain why my father, when he came to England on leave in 1913 and was looking for a school for me, thought I might feel more at home if I were to have as my companions other boys with an Indian background, who spoke, as it were, the same language.

The educational agency which he consulted directed him to St. Cyprian's and there, after a short spell as a day boy, I found myself a boarder at the end of 1913. I did not have the impression, then or later, that the school had a particularly strong Indian connection. There were boys who had been born in India or their fathers were employed there, such as Eric Blair, the Kirkpatricks and Rivett-Carnac - a good Anglo-Indian name - but there was no tendency for young 'koi hais' to congregate, and any showing off by airing one's Hindustani was not encouraged.

The school had been in existence for about ten years, and I suppose it had eighty or so boys in 1913. The headmaster, Leslie Vaughan Wilkes and his wife Cecily - Sambo and Flip to many generations of boys - presided in tandem. Unlike in temperament, they complemented each other effectively in teaching and administration, which were of a kind appropriate to that late imperial period, before the decline.

It was an excellent school of its kind, with a growing reputation; my father could not have chosen better for me. I may not always have thought so, especially in my first months as a day boy, when I used to creep unwillingly along Summerdown Road, looking for crystals in the flint walls to prolong the journey. Not that my schoolfellows were particularly unkind to me; nor were they invariably kind. They would hide my cap and upset my books and pull me by the leg along the polished passage floors. But I was not the only victim; such indignities are the lot of all small boys, at whatever school, until they grow large enough to discourage them.

I was at St.Cyprian's for seven years, astride the years of the First World War. For this reason, and for others, unconnected with the school, they were years of light and shade. I can remember, as can every schoolboy, spells of acute misery and loneliness; but I was young and resilient. I grew in stature, in spite of wartime rationing: I learned to run and box, shoot and play the drum, (I even won the silver drumsticks in the school bugle band, a tribute to Lakshman's earlier coaching). I was made to acquire, not without discomfort, the habit of exercising the muscles of the mind, like those of the body, until it hurt if need be; a habit which if not acquired by the age of twelve, may be lost for ever in the tide of adolescence. For me the years at St. Cyprian's were, on the whole happy years.

Some of my contemporaries, destined for distinction, would not have agreed with me. Cyril Connolly, critic and author in later years, mocked the old-fashioned discipline and methods of teaching; and Eric Blair (George Orwell) wrote, long after he had left the school, in terms of bitter resentment at the inferiority he was made to feel of being a poor boy among rich men's sons. There were at St. Cyprian's in our time two sons of peers and a Siamese prince. The Siamese was a good rugby

St. Cyprian's, Eastbourne

Mrs. C.V. Wilkes of St. Cyprian's, 1921

player, but otherwise they were not superior, rather unremarkable characters not such as to cause the complex of which Blair complained. There may have been boys whose fathers owned grouse moors or yachts, but we did not hear of them. There were more boys of the same family background as Eric Blair and myself. In my case the comparison is apt. We had both been born in India, where our fathers were serving; we both clashed with authority and were punished, but I was never conscious of snobbery or discrimination, - of unfairness sometimes, because school justice is rough, and what schoolboy does not feel it? We were both well taught, and sent with scholarships to our public schools - and later, in our turn, to serve in the East.

Whatever may have been the cause of the outsize chip which Blair-Orwell carried on his shoulder throughout his life, I doubt if it was school experience. Indeed I have evidence to the contrary. I corresponded once with a lady who had known him well in his Burmese days. She quoted him as expressing his gratitude to the schools that had trained him, especially for the avoidance of prejudice and the capacity to think for himself.

For this Cicely Vaughan Wilkes, 'Flip', would have been mainly responsible. She was a remarkable woman by any standard. She had five splendid children of her own, but her real family was St.Cyprian's, the many hundreds of boys for whom, generation after generation, she was an elemental force of nature. She had an ample figure and small deep-set eyes in a broad face, which could light up and shake with laughter or cloud over and tremble with rage, within the hour. She was Saraswati, Ganesh and Kali rolled into one. No primitive farmers ever scanned the omens of the sky more anxiously, to divine the mood of the Earth Mother, than we watched for changes in the climate of Flip's grace and geniality.

She was an inspired teacher of history and English, and a stern disciplinarian, not only of manners and behaviour, but of taste in reading and style in writing. She encouraged us to read poetry and to learn it by heart, and to try our hand at writing verse. If our compositions were found worthy, we were rewarded by seeing them published in the school 'Chronicle'; and sometimes we might be stood up on summer evenings in the garden, in front of long-suffering parents, to recite Gray's Elegy or Keats' Ode to a Nightingale. I was once surprised, and rather gratified to observe, while so engaged, that I seemed to have reduced one parent to tears. Of course, it may only have been hay fever.

Flip was matriarchal and unpredictable and, like Rudyard Kipling's character, we 'learned about women from her'; and we learned much else besides. Greek irregular verbs may have been knocked into our heads (with a heavy silver pencil) by Sambo, her husband; but most of the rest of what it took to win a place in College at Eton, three of us, at any rate, Connolly, Blair-Orwell and Christie, owed to Flip.

*   *   *   *   *

It took two attempts for me to become a Tug. The first had been a near miss; the examiners gave some weightage in marks for candidates of the tender age of twelve, but in my case it had not been quite enough. I had scraped onto the select list, but the vacancies of that year among the seventy poor scholars whom King Henry the Sixth has endowed to sing masses for his soul at the King's College of Our Lady of Eton beside Windsor, did not reach down to me. In the summer of 1919, at the riper age of thirteen, I had another try and, to the intense relief of all concerned, managed to secure a place. When, a few months later, the Provost laid his hand benignly on my head and pronounced in Latin the formula "Be a good boy, docile and truthful ", I was admitted to the Foundation, a little Tug.

A Tug because 'togatus', a gowned one. King's Scholars or Collegers, our proper designation, wore gowns in school and white surplices in Chapel. The gowns had vulnerable long, loose sleeves which young Oppidans, if they could not knock off one's top hat, would tweak and run away, shouting "Tug,Tug".

Oppidans were, literally, town boys, satellites of the Foundation, whose parents had, since the Middle Ages, recognised the merits of the place, and sent them with tutors to boarding houses in the town, so that they might share the advantages of the education. Some of the boarding-house keepers had graduated to the authority of house-mistresses, or Dames, and the last and greatest of them, Dame Evans, survived into my own lifetime. Her house colours had been scarlet with black skull and cross bones formidable on the playing field. The colour of College was royal purple.

There were about eleven hundred Oppidans, boarded in twenty-four houses, and they were apt to regard the seventy Collegers as a race apart; but familiarity bred mutual respect, for the Collegers could hold their own at games, and also had other uses. They were, by definition, 'saps' and could sometimes be persuaded by an Oppidan who had not prepared his work, to sock him the construe on the way to school.

Much of this was known to me by the report of others who had gone before. I was ready for it, and even looked forward to it.

> "Alas! regardless of their doom,
> The little victims play -"

sang Thomas Gray, in his Ode on a Distant Prospect of Eton College. I had no such forebodings at my first sight of the grey chapel rising from the water-meadows curtailed in its grand design by the Wars of the Roses; the mellow red brick of the older medieval buildings, even the garish brick of the nineteenth century New Buildings; the cobblestones of School Yard, the statue of King Henry, Lupton's Tower and the Cloisters.

In Gray's time, I suppose, a young Colleger might have quailed, had he known, at what awaited him in Long Chamber, a barrack overlooking School Yard into which all the scholars used to be locked at night, and spent much of it in rat hunts, tossing in the blanket, squib fights and other such riotous pursuits.

Long Chamber is no more, but it was a place of character when I first knew it in 1920. It preserved much of its independence, but had also acquired some latter-day respectability. It was a self-governing colony, insulated by Sixth Form Passage and the Master-in-College's quarters had its own Captain of Chamber, its own customs, laws, sanctions and rights, including the precious right of privacy.

Each boy had his own cubicle, called a stall, with a folding box bed, a 'burry' - desk and wardrobe combined - a basin with a cold tap, a hot-water can, a shallow tin bath tub and a 'siphon', about four feet of rubber tubing whereby water from the basin could be siphoned into the bath. The siphon was also an instrument of execution in the hands of the Captain of Chamber. In my time the Captain of Chamber was Godfrey Meynell, later to win a posthumous V.C. on the North West Frontier of India.

The stalls had no doors, but red curtains which were left open if the occupant felt sociable, but drawn to shut out the rest of the world if he felt studious or private. If one were to invade this privacy uninvited, the owner could invoke an ancient right. Like a Channel Islander who can still call effectively for justice on the successors of Duke William of Normandy, by crying: "Haro! A mon aide, mon prince", an aggrieved stallholder could shout, with reasonable pauses, "Stall curtains! Stall curtains!" The Captain of Chamber was then obliged after satisfying himself that the call was not frivolous, to inflict summary punishment with his own piece of rubber tubing; and that could be more painful than it sounds.

Life in a boy's first year at a public school is very full, far too full to allow time for serious consideration of how, nine or ten years later he is to earn his living. So far I had certainly not been committed to the idea of returning to India, but I can remember vividly the moment when the idea was first caused to take shape.

It arose out of a curious and irrelevant incident - my first fight with a fellow new boy. The cause was no doubt trivial, but the fight was real enough, with bare fists and in hot blood, in more senses than one, for it took place on a warm Sunday afternoon. We fought grimly and noisily all over the open space in the middle of Long Chamber, giving and taking punishment for about a quarter of an hour, until we had both had enough, and the Chapel bell for evensong reminded me that I had another engagement. Here my opponent had an advantage, for he was a Roman Catholic: he had already been to Mass, and the Chapel bell meant nothing to him. We hurriedly and insincerely shook hands; I struggled into my surplice and reached my place in Chapel by the narrowest of margins, just in front of 'The Ram', the processional entry of the Sixth Form. There I stood and sang and prayed, for one of the most uncomfortable hours I have ever spent, robed in white but scarlet in the face, while the steam ascended from me like a column of smoke from a burnt offering.

Strangely, my condition drew only one comment from higher authority. The Biology master stopped me outside Chapel.

"Boy", he said, "you seem to perspire very freely. You should do well in a hot climate. Go east, boy, go east."

It was good advice, and some years later I took it.

The first year or two in College were the salad days, when the pressure of work and games was comparatively light. We were adjusting ourselves to the new disciplines and learning to organise our time, for we had a deceptive amount of free time into which allotted tasks had to be fitted, at our own judgement and peril. We were finding our friends and forming those first vivid impressions which would stay with us through our lives; impressions of simple things, sights sounds and smells which clutch at the mind whenever a whiff or echo of them floats by.

Particularly smells; the smell of rotting water-weed in the river, of chestnut candles on Upper Club, of mud and sweat and a suspicion of drains in a Wall Game bully; of lilac in Judy's Passage; of Thames Valley fog drifting into gas-lit class-rooms at early school; of sausages frying for Sunday breakfast. Before we could get at these, however, there was a short service of Latin prayers and hymns to be got through.

Rex Henricus - Sis amicus -
(we sang to our Founder Saint and King)
Nobis in angustia -
but the only 'Angst' of which we were conscious was the gnawing

13

hunger of a growing boy.

We were growing up as well as growing. College was inevitably a forcing house; the competition of our fellows, and the prospect of some examination or other always in the offing, kept us to the mark. The young Oppidan had only to avoid disaster; we were expected to achieve distinction. The pressure was mercifully tempered by the tutorial system. Every boy had his own Tutor, distinct from his House Tutor (who, in our case, was the Master-in-College) and from the 'beaks', masters who taught him in school. This survival from the days when boys came to Eton accompanied by their own family tutors, meant that every boy had a personnel guardian-pedagogue, an extra taskmaster, vigilant of his progress, but a confidant and advocate in time of trouble, and whose special care it was to see that his pupil's mind was exposed to wider interests outside the school curriculum.

The quality of the teaching was unsurpassed. I think we realised that even as boys. The secret weapon which most of our teachers had in common, with variations, was the appeal to the imagination which drew out the mind. Nevertheless, the framework of our teaching had hardly changed from that of the nineteenth century. Whatever aberrations into history, mathematics or even science we might choose when the time came to specialise, we could not escape (Deo gratias) the thorough early grounding in Horace and Homer, which was still the foundation of every gentleman's education.

The classics, in College, permeated our daily lives. We prayed and sang and said grace in Latin, and even the graffiti in the lavatories showed a classical influence. Every Colleger knew, of course, that the Cloaca Maxima was the main drain of imperial Rome. Ronald Knox, who was a wit and versifier before he was a Monsignor, discovered its tutelary spirit, whom he invoked:

> Fair Cloacina, goddess of this place,
> Th'accustomed seat of every child of grace,
> Soft o'er thy throne may our libations flow,
> Not rudely swift nor obstinately slow.

A liberal tradition, however, allowed plenty of gaps in the ancient structure for the winds of change to blow through; and in the early twenties they were blowing strongly.

It could hardly have been otherwise. The war was over, and young men who might have been in the trenches now found themselves at the top of the school, with an unexpected lease of life, and time to think and question the basis of a system which had gone far towards extinguishing a whole generation of their seniors. Rebellion, of a kind, was in the air, but a comparatively modest intellectual rebellion of adolescents, protesters against established order, in whose company to confess a taste for Rudyard Kipling would draw shouts of 'Imperialist!' - 'Reactionary!' and worse.

The unrest did not last long because there was always so much else, outside the ample routine of work and games, to distract our minds from any prolonged sense of social or political grievance. A common feature of most King's Scholars, then and now, is a tendency to many-sidedness. There was no explicit encouragement to combine 'sapping' - hard book work, which was taken for granted - with other interests, or particularly with athletic endeavour; but there was in College an unexpressed assumption of the importance of being as complete a man as possible - of combining 'cum Minerva Martem'. It was the classical ideal.

And it was the Wall Game, I suppose, which played the most important part in our collective athletic emotions. At any given time there are probably as many Collegers who heartily detest that primitive, illogical form of football as are enthusiasts for it; but the fact that, once a year, the pick of seventy King's Scholars are matched against the pick of eleven hundred Oppidans at the Wall, provides the bond of a seemingly unequal contest against a common adversary that any minority needs to preserve its vigour and solidarity.

Old Collegers have gone into battle wearing their Wall colours, and Collegers solemnly drink a loving cup once a year in pious memory of James Kenneth Stephen, outstanding player and poet of the game. Like any Oppidans, Collegers dressed themselves up as Regency bucks, with flowered waistcoats, silver-topped canes and tassels, at Lords; or in the fancy sailor suits of George III's navy for the Procession of Boats on The Fourth of June; but that crude and uncomfortable mudlark at the Wall is the Collegers' own game, and no doubt will continue to be so, as long as the brick wall divides College Field from the Slough Road.

Even the irreverent, sardonic shade of George Orwell probably remembers with secret pride that he was one of the very few who have contrived the scoring of a goal in the Wall Game.

* * * * *

I had no doubt about where I wanted to go after Eton, and when I was lucky enough to be offered, with a year in hand, a place at Eton's sister foundation, King's College, Cambridge, I resigned the tempting glories of a few more months at school and grabbed the opportunity. It was exhilarating to step out of adolescence. We had already been treated at school as responsible people, entrusted with organising our own time and by no means discouraged from voicing our opinions or following our own legitimate ploys: but in the adult university world liberty seemed to be enhanced an hundredfold. The obligations and restraints of discipline, such as they were, were light and easily borne. We were consulted rather than bidden - though I daresay with a little guiding pressure - about what lectures we should attend and what books we should read. The Tripos, which brought its own compulsions later, was still distant.

King's was in some ways an exceptional college. It's chapel is the perpendicular glory of Europe, and the choral scholars who filled it with song, endowed the college with a strong musical tradition.

'Beauty is Truth, Truth Beauty'. The pursuit of truth is the proper aim of all study, and beauty in the sights and sounds we lived with was a powerful aid to the unfolding of our minds. We were fortunate, too, in the senior members of the College, the dons, our supervisors and lecturers, with whom there was close and easy communication. They impressed on us, as soon as we arrived, that we were as fully members of the University as they, the only distinction being that the senior members had a function to teach us what they knew, if we were ready to learn. They were a good vintage; of classical scholars, mathematicians, economists, historians. Among them was Maynard Keynes, the Bursar, who commuted between Bloomsbury and Cambridge; there was John Sheppard, impressario of the Greek Plays, whose lectures were a theatrical performance, and F.E. Adcock, Professor of Ancient History, whose wit and erudition, modestly offered to us with an irresistible lisp in crowded lecture halls were often drowned by the thunderous applause of undergraduate feet.

I had the good fortune to occupy the same rooms in Kings for four years, overlooking the river and the 'Backs'. They were kept superficially tidy by my bedmaker, Mrs Nightingale, who called me 'my gentleman with the hobburn 'air' (I had reddish hair, and was called 'Red' by my contemporaries). She exacted tribute for the compliment, for her capacious carpet bag always seemed to be bulging when she went off duty, and my supply of coal and butter and tea diminished regularly, but not too obviously, at a rate above that of my own consumption.

This was in keeping with a kind of platonic communism in matters of property which was practised in Cambridge at that time, and is probably still practised. There was a convention which regarded food, drink, tobacco, bicycles, gowns, even privacy (unless one sported one's oak, - closed the outer door, - which was done sparingly, and only in the exigencies of work) as at the disposal of one's neighbours - on a reciprocal basis, of course. KOINA TA TÔN PHILÔN - the property of friends is common, said the classical scholars; while GNOTHI SEAUTON said the dons, know yourself, find out what you are and be yourself; 'do your own thing' they might say today. It was a good advice, and the best of precepts for a university education.

My first three years at Cambridge were crowded and exciting, and seem in retrospect, to have flashed by. I read classics for the first part of the Tripos and changed to modern history for the second. I frequented the running track at Fenners, and even helped Cambridge to win the University Relay Races. I was continuously and romantically in love (with an innocence unimaginable today). Concerts, theatres, societies, interminable undergraduate discussions - these were also fitted in, and Long Vacations spent partly in travel and partly in serious reading. The General Strike of 1926 faced us, briefly, with political reality, and caused some of us, led by me as an amateur police sergeant to be transported to Whitechapel as a special constabulary reserve.

At some point in my third year I decided, after considering various alternatives and listening to some persuasive arguments - not least from my old headmaster of St Cyprian's - to sit for the Indian Civil Service examination in August. India, I suppose was written on my forehead: I do not expect I needed much persuading. But after I had finished the Tripos in May it was a daunting prospect to spend the next three months preparing for another ordeal, consisting of more than twenty three-hour papers, covering a range of subjects wider than the Tripos.

At this juncture the tempter whispered in my ear, in the shape of W.H. Macaulay, Vice-Provost of King's. He had family connections with a well-established firm of merchants in India, and he suggested that, subject to interview, they might offer me a lucrative post, with a fourth year at Cambridge thrown in for good measure.

It was tantalising. An interview was arranged, and I made my way to an obscure corner of the City of London, where I was pleasantly received by the Directors. They did not ask many questions, but were concerned to impress on me what an interesting and prosperous future awaited me if I should join their firm, and reach their age and eminence. They talked among themselves, perhaps for my benefit, about their yachts and deer forests; and then, almost as an afterthought, they offered me employment. They also made it clear that I must make up my mind quickly; I could not keep their offer in my pocket while I sat for the I.C.S. I was sorely tempted. India, on which I had set my heart, whould still be my destination, and was a bird in hand, without the imminent sweat and tears.

But I think my mind was already made up. The next day I

wrote to thank them and said that I had decided to take the examination. Then the real generosity of those Directors appeared. They replied that they could understand my decision, and wished me luck; but they also wished me to know that if, by any chance, things should go amiss, their offer remained open.

This was a very present help in the tribulations of the next few weeks when, with hundreds of candidates in the combined examination for the Home and Indian Civil Services, the Colonial Service and the Eastern Cadetships, I was toiling away in Burlington Gardens through an August heat wave. Day after day we spilled ourselves onto paper, hour after scorching hour; and, on the hour, we would sigh and sit back, laying down our pens until the carillon of Atkinson's scent shop in Bond Street should have finished chiming out an air from 'The Beggars Opera".

By the end of this marathon we were so exhausted that we hardly cared what the result might be. One of my fellow candidates from Cambridge was a Bengali who had an original mind and a passion for physical fitness, which he indulged by running five miles every day and sparring with professional boxers. Towards the end of the examination, however, he was depressed and certain that he had failed. He confided to me that his parents had spent so much on his education that, having failed, he could not face them again. He had discovered, somewhere in London, a recruiting office for the French Foreign Legion, and had applied to join it. He had been supplied with forms to complete and papers about the conditions of service; but, wisely, the recruiting officer had suggested that he should think over the prospect and return after a week. I advised him to wait at least until the examination results were out. It was well that he did so, for otherwise Calcutta would have been deprived in later years of one of its best Chief Presidency Magistrates, while Ranjit Gupta, in the uniform of Beau Geste, might have been helping garrison some fort in the Sahara. My fourth year at King's, as a graduate and Indian Civil Service probationer, was carefree in the sense that I enjoyed an excuse for being a good deal less industrious than I had been for years, and enjoyed being paid for it too. Indian probationers, recruited in India, were sent to British universities for two years; we British recruits were the gainers from meeting and getting to know them, but I now believe that we would have gained more if we had been required to spend our probationary year in India, where we would have learned law in the courts of the country and languages from the lips of the people. However, that did not occur to me at the time; I took my riding lessons more seriously than I did my instruction in Indian law, languages and history.

It suddenly became important, as the days slipped past, and

became tinged with the sadness of approaching good-byes, to squeeze every drop of worthwhile experience and pleasure out of the company of one's friends and of the country which one would only see again at long intervals in the unimaginable duration of a working life. Some of us would not see it again. Arthur Luce of King's who sailed with me to India, died while working in a famine camp at Gonda, in the United Provinces, before a year had passed.

I.C.S. probationers, Cambridge, 1928 (part of group). (Left to right; back row E.S. Hyde, K.N. Nagarkatti, standing G. Burgess, M.R. Sachdev, M. Karamatullah, D.C. Majumdar, sitting W.H.J. Christie, J.S. Mallanah, Mr. H.F. Samman (tutor), squatting A.H. Kemp)

3
Bengal Paddy

The dark ship ploughs the emerald fires of foam....
my scarcely adult Muse began to put words to a nostalgic
sentiment -
  ...and westward sink the memories of home.
    Plough on, you senseless funeral, why so slow?
    You carry those that know not why they go.

I was leaning over the stern of the P & O 'Rawalpindi'
watching the phosphorescent wake, somewhere in the Indian Ocean.
I was leaving my heart behind me, it is true; but otherwise,
even making allowance for the melancholy of evening, the
sentiment was false. I knew well enough where and why I was
going. It was in December, 1928. I was not yet twenty-three,
and I was joining my first post in the Indian Civil Service.
The 'Rawalpindi' - which, eleven years later, was to go down
defending her convoy gallantly against enemy warships - was then
conveying, as an insignificant part of a distinguished passenger
list which included Maharajahs, Generals and Commissioners, a
few of us I.C.S. 'griffins' to India. I had been posted to
Bengal.
    Among my fellow passengers was Philip Mason, who later,
alias Philip Woodruff, was to be the historian of our Service.
He had passed in top of the list, and had chosen the United
Provinces. I had passed second. We had all been asked to name
three provinces in order of our preference for posting. I had
put Punjab first - an automatic preference for most candidates -
then the United Provinces - adjacent to the Punjab, the heart of
Aryavarta, land of the Two Rivers and many fine cities - and
then I hesitated. I really knew very little about India,
although I had been born there. My father had served in the
104th Wellesley Rifles, a Mahratta regiment, and I had been born
in Shivaji's capital, Poona. I suppose that made me a
Maharasthrian, and I should have named Bombay as one of my
choices; but at Cambridge I had heard a compelling lecture
from, I think, a member of the Butler family, whose theme had
been the historical interest and importance of Bengal, so much
more important than our other 'factories' and settlements in

India. "Had not" (he asked rhetorically) "our whole Indian Empire grown from the need to protect, not the precarious footholds in Madras or Bombay, but our possessions in Bengal - from the days of Job Charnock's pestilential encampment on the banks of the Hooghly, from the tribulations and heroism of Fort William, enriched later by Clive's jagir of the 24 Pergannahs - just as the British Empire itself had grown from, and British foreign policy and strategy had for two centuries been dictated by the need to protect our Indian Empire?"

As a small camp-follower, I knew the Punjab. I remembered Ambala, and the crisp winter mornings of northern India; the journeys by mule-drawn tonga from the plains to the aromatic freshness of the pines in Mrs. Hawksbee's Simla; the monkeys on Jakko, and the distant Himalayan snows. I had seen some of the pageantry of the 1911 Coronation Durbar in Delhi, where my father had been on duty. Yes, I was sure about Punjab as my first choice, and I would probably get it, if Mason succeeded with his own choice of the United Provinces. Third choice probably would not matter anyway; I might as well put down Bengal. But it did matter. Bengal was not a popular posting in those days, and I was probably one of the few who had put it anywhere on their list. So for Bengal I was bound: I never regretted it.

I knew why I was going for another reason. The Indian Civil Service, we were told, was a career 'open to the talents' with high traditions of service, not primarily as servants of the ruling power, but of the nearly five-hundred million people of the then undivided India and Burma, among whom we would be working. We were the senior administrative service, the chosen few, only eleven hundred of us, about equally divided between British and Indian. Some were chair-borne in judges' courts or secretariats; some were in the Political Service, attached to Princes' States or on the North-West Frontier or in the Persian Gulf; and the rest, a really select band, were District Officers of various grades and denominations, simultaneously Magistrates (to administer the law) and Collectors (to administer the rights of land tenure and its revenue). We should remain in the provinces of our original posting unless and until it pleased almighty Delhi to summon us to the Central Government, a fate from which our provincial seniors would strenuously fight to preserve us; or, if accidentally they had let us go, would later try to rescue us.

It was a prestigious service, and most of us believed in those days that we were following a vocation, not just a career. That sounds presumptuous, but it was true. I acknowledge the merits and achievements of sister Services, modelled on the I.C.S., in other parts of the Empire, but loyalty forbids me to allow that they equalled our own. Never had there been, never perhaps will there be again, such a Service. Plato's trained rulers were a philosopher's dream, but the Indian Civil Service was a reality, and our Indian colleagues took, and still take as much pride in it as ourselves. No wonder that we should be called, by mocking compatriots, the Heaven-born, the White Brahmins, neither Indian nor civil nor servants, incorruptible but unapproachable. The last epithet was not quite fair; for we would be taught the virtue of accessibility, whether on horseback, in camp, in court or in our houses, and it cost some their lives. But the habit of impartiality bred a measure of aloofness, a reluctance to mix too freely, say in the club bar with those who might be appearing before us in court the following day.

Not only had the Service prestige; by the standards of those days, the pay was also good. We started on about £400 a year, and after twenty-five years service we could retire, at the unimaginably advanced age of forty-seven or so, on a princely full pension of £1000. 1928 + 25 = 1953. That was in the misty future: there was no point in looking so far ahead.

Meanwhile the present was with us as we stepped ashore at Bombay to go our several ways; and the present brought us down a peg or two. In a few days time we should all be 'stunt sahibs' - the lowest form of life in the Service - assistant magistrates and collectors in our various districts, invested with the minumum powers until we had passed more examinations.

I was posted to Mymensingh District in eastern Bengal, which is now Bangladesh. It was the largest district in the Presidency of Fort William and probably the largest in India - larger than Wales, both in area and population. It was one of several districts of the Dacca Division. The old course of the Brahmaputra river flowed diagonally across it, and the extreme flatness of the country was relieved only in the north by the outline of the Garo Hills in Assam.

Jute and paddy were the main, practically the only crops, but there was no monotony in the countryside. Innumerable villages, hidden in thickets of bamboo, the changing colours and height of the crops, the quality of the light reflected from great sheets of water, and continually moving cloud patterns all helped to beguile the senses. The paddy varied from the brilliant green of the seedlings along river banks to the pale yellow of the ripened grain, in two harvests a year. The jute grew in six months from seedling to a seven-foot stalk, and, such excellent cover did the crop afford for a fugitive wrong-doer, that the incidence of crime grew with it. The jute was cut in September, after the rains, and lay 'retting' or rotting in ditches everywhere, an offence to the nose, until it was taken away to be processed into the silky, silver-gold fibre, the wealth of East Bengal.

The Collector of Mymensingh was Cyril Gurner, a fine administrator with a touch of eccentricity, which often makes the best. I had telegraphed to him from Calcutta: 'Have bought gun shall I bring horse?', to which he replied, 'Can it swim?'. Whoever had told me that shooting, riding and bridge were almost obligatory for the young civilian, had neglected to warn me that East Bengal is watery at all times, and becomes an inland sea for four months of the year.

Cyril and Phyllis Gurner took me into their house and their family, and gave me the best introduction to India that any 'stunt' could wish for. Cyril Gurner was a Sanskrit scholar, donnish in appearance and manner, but as we cycled to the office together on the morning after I had arrived, he was severely practical.

'How much Bengali can you speak?' I told him that, at Cambridge, we had learned from a gramophone record King Edward VII's coronation speech, translated into formal Sanskritised Bengali.

'Repeat some of it'. He stopped me after a few lines.

'That would be about as useful here as asking an Irishman the way to Tipperary in the language of Paradise Lost. Forget it, and try to pick up Mymensingh Bengali as quickly as you can - though, I warn you, it will not help you to be understood in Calcutta. As to court work, do not try to carry the law and procedure in your head; your bench clerk will steer you, and you will soon pick up the practice of the courts. By the way, I am going to throw you in at the deep end: you shall try your first case today. Don't worry; there will be no miscarriage of justice. Whatever your decision, there will be an appeal against it. But try not to let the pleaders argue in English; it costs their clients more, and you miss a free lesson in the local dialect.'

My court room appeared to be part of a converted cowshed - good enough, I suppose, for a third class magistrate - and, appropriately, my first case was one of cattle trespass. In the middle of the third afternoon the accused's pleader was still droning on, in scarcely intelligible English, having foiled, by threats to apply for a transfer of the case - which I felt would be the ultimate disgrace - all my efforts to make him speak Bengali. Only he and I were awake when a cow put her head round the open door and took a mouthful of the case records off the sleeping bench-clerk's table. The bench-clerk woke with a shout, and the resulting hue and cry emptied my court-room, and several others near by, more quickly than an earthquake. The cow was cornered, but the records were not recovered intact. However, justice of a sort was probably done without them.

The Mymensingh station club was a small single-storeyed building, but large enough for its dozen members, with three rooms, for bridge, billiards and the bar. My predecessor in the post of assistant magistrate had given me valuable advice.
'Do you play bridge?' he asked.
'Yes, after a fashion.'
'If you value your freedom, do not admit it. Once it is known, you will become a slave. There will always be three bridge players lying in wait for you to make the fourth. Every evening they will send a club servant to fetch you, as soon as you get back from the office, while you are still in your bath.'
I took his advice, declined all offers to teach me the game, and concentrated on snooker and the bar.
One evening, some weeks after I had arrived, I witnessed a piece of drama in the club. The various games had finished, and members were preparing to go home to their dinners. A barman with a tray of drinks offered one to the civil surgeon's wife.
'Which sahib ordered this?' she asked.
'The police sahib.'
She rose with the glass in her hand, walked to the edge of the verandah, and threw the whisky out into the night.
'Tell that to the police sahib!' she said.
I was impressed: it might have been a scene out of the Mrs. Hawksbee saga, or from 'A Passage to India'. I enquired later what it was all about.
'Very little,' I was told, 'there are always station feuds: they are not serious, and they don't last long. Some women would have no excitement in their lives without them. But take care not to get involved yourself.'
I was too occupied for that; and the small official and business community, British, Bengali, Anglo-Indian and the Greek jute merchant's family across the river, were kind and hospitable, after I had dropped my visiting cards dutifully in their 'Not At Home' boxes. They were tolerant of my callowness, helpful with my problems and full of good advice.
'Don't be afraid of making mistakes', they said. 'Learn by experience; above all, get out into the country, mix with the people, pick up the language.'
I was steered through the labyrinth of Collectorate offices by patient Bengali deputy collectors. I cycled over miles of intricate village roads, earth tracks on top of high paddy bunds, inspecting Union Boards (newly established instruments of local self-government), markets, dispensaries and schools. I

was charged with the after-care of youthful ex-convicts. I dealt with miscellaneous correspondence - I suspect the Collector passed to me the more answerable letters - including, for example, a peremptory demand that several coffins, prematurely ordered from the Public Works Department, and lying unused in their godowns for over two years, 'should be put to use forthwith.'

Some of my duties were grim. A magistrate had to witness and certify death after a hanging in the district jail. I had to do it, but only once. It was very early in the morning. The civil surgeon was with me, and took a good look at me.

'I have to go and see that he is dead,' he said, 'but if you care to take my word for it and sign....' I did.

Winter had brought the snipe into the paddy lands and jheels, and I found that pursuit of that elusive quarry was another excuse for getting out into the countryside at week-ends. It was considered poor shooting if one expended more than two cartridges per bird; but I did not mind too much about my average, so long as I could bring two or three couple triumphantly home for breakfast. I soon learned not to stand still for more than a few seconds in knee-deep water. The first time I did so, there was a ring of elephant leeches round the top of my stocking, feasting on my blood.

One day two deputations of young Bengalis called on me in succession, each with a football shirt of different colour in their hands, and asked me to play for their team in a friendly match. I accepted gratefully the invitation of the first-comers. At the time appointed there was a larger crowd of spectators than I had expected; then I realised that the centre of attraction was myself, the only European and the only booted player on the field. This was embarrassing, as I was not a star performer, and my bare-footed opponents were soon making rings round me. It was even more embarrassing to find that, if I did come into physical contact with a light-weight Bengali, the rebound alone was likely to send him flying, to the accompaniment of shouts of indignation from the touch line, and whistle for a foul. Whenever I measured my length in the mud, the crowd were overjoyed. I found it uncomfortable to be an instrument for the release of racial tensions, though I understood what they felt, and the players themselves were friendly.

'Careful how you go', I was warned in the club. 'Those teams may call themselves Mymensingh Sporting and the Friends Eleven, but they represent the Anushilan and the Jugantar respectively, both revolutionary parties, the main difference being that the Jugantar are assassins too.' I do not suppose I influenced those footballers' political ideas, but they certainly helped to improve my colloquial Bengali.

Bengal was a strange soil for terrorism to grow in - a soft country, inhabited by a gentle, intelligent and talkative race. 'We are sweet-toothed and fish-eating,' they would admit disarmingly, 'and therefore a very fearful people.' Other Indians found little to admire in them except their sweets, their music and the beauty of their women. I can hardly explain the strong attraction which I came to feel for Bengal and the Bengalis, for much that happened there in the next few years was not easy to forgive. But in that first innocent year, in the fields and villages and towns of Mymensingh district, some magic was at work which binds me still. There were so many ingredients of the spell, sounds, sights and smells, some remembered, more forgotten. A child herding water-buffaloes; the grace of women carrying pitchers from the well; the modest twitch of a _sari_ across a face, leaving one eye uncovered for curiosity; a young man striding behind a plough or poised on a boat to spear a fish; the dignity of grey-bearded elders distilling the wisdom of generations under an ancient tree; the caress of deep bamboo shade in the heat of the day; the smell of thirsty dust in the wind of approaching rain; the stinging smoke of burning cow-dung cakes, the rich savours of ghee frying or corn roasting; the sound of cattle bells, and the slow movement of returning herds; the cries and flares and excitement of a bazaar at night; the drums of a distant wedding. Such were the impressions that I continued to absorb wherever in India I might be, so that they are now part of a reservoir of sensory experience accumulated over the years - from which, curiously, the less pleasant impressions seem to have filtered out. It is a loss to be deprived of that experience, and when I can taste it again there is a quickening of the pulse.

Before I left Mymensingh, a Bengali Collector had assumed charge of the district. He was a man of many parts, an expert in folk dancing and folk verse, and had even published a collection of Bengali limericks. He made me converse with him in Bengali, but not before it was almost too late. I have a good ear, and the Bengali which I had already picked up in the bazaar, on the football field and from my _munshi_, a Collectorate clerk who had never been outside the district, was not Bengali as it is spoken in Calcutta.

The result was that when I sat for the Departmental Examinations in Calcutta, my criminal and revenue law were found to be satisfactory, and I could read and write Bengali, but in the _viva voce_ test I baffled the examiners. There are half-a-dozen dialects of the language, and those of East Bengal are particularly broad.

'Can anyone understand what this man is saying?' the chief examiner asked his collegues.

'Yes I think I can,' said a retired judge, an East Bengal man from Dacca. 'Let me speak with him in his own tongue.'

After a few exchanges he said, 'We may pass him. He can speak Bengali of a sort: but he should polish his accent and his idiom before he is posted to a civilised district.'

The next four winter months were spent under canvas, in Settlement Training Camp. This, in retrospect, was an idyllic period of one's service in India - the last months before real responsibility descended on us. Of my first-year colleagues in Bengal four were Indian and two British, and we were now assembled from our various districts to take part in the long-term, perpetually revolving exercise which is one of the great legacies to India of British rule: the careful mapping, recording of tenancy rights and fixing of revenue for every tiny field in the vast patchwork of land tenures throughout the sub-continent.

Our camp was in West Bengal, not far from the battlefield of Plassey. With plane-table and chain, with volumes of records, we went to the villages, fixed boundaries, settled disputes, learning and carrying out the various stages of Settlement, which had fine Persian names - kistwar, buhjarat, jamabandi. In our spare time we shot snipe and duck for the pot, and explored the countryside. One day we came upon a leopardess with two cubs, asleep in a nullah. The villagers asked us to kill her, as she was taking toll of their goats. We excused ourselves, and tip-toed away from that encounter, regardless of the face we lost, as we had nothing more lethal than sharp pencils with us at the time. We made up for it another day by shooting a crocodile which had been monopolising a village tank for some time, and depriving the village ladies of their laundry and bathing place.

The idyll was over far too soon. Now we were fully fledged, and judged fit for an independent charge. Not quite independent, however, I was posted as Sub-Divisional Officer of Asansol. Keeping a watchful eye on me from sixty miles away would be the District Magistrate of Burdwan, and over him the Commissioner, even more remote. Asansol is in the extreme west of Bengal, on the Bihar border, and I was proud of my new charge as if I were monarch of all I surveyed.

It was good country, with bone in it: rocks and low hills, cold in winter, hell-fire in summer; a change from the river silt and paddy fields of East Bengal. There was a rich seam of coal running through its western end, and there was iron ore in the hills of Bihar. The area therefore included many collieries

Settlement training, Bengal, 1930

and a number of industries, among them two great iron and steel works. This added an industrial element to the normal incidents of administration, considerations of labour relations, safety regulations and factory laws.

The main problems, however, at the time, all over Bengal, were the civil disobedience movement and a serious outbreak of terrorism. At a time when I should have been accumulating normal administrative experience, I found myself concerned mainly with the abnormal business of discouraging and reducing the opportunities for riot and mayhem, officially called preservation of law and order. I soon learnt that bluff and a sense of humour, if one could keep and use it, were the most effective unofficial instruments. I was fortunate in having, in the superintendent of police, a colleague of my own age and the same bent towards unorthodoxy. We decided that, if we were to keep the peace, in a civilised way, we should have to depart from the rule book.

One of the first objects of all political rebels is to court punishment and martyrdom: but I refused to fill the jail with schoolboys, however anxious they might have been to earn the jail qualification of a freedom fighter. We descended on groups of young patriots who were breaking the law in the easiest possible way, by picketing liquor shops, piled them into police buses - after their weeping families had garlanded them - and drove away. Later we dropped them off, one by one, at nightfall in the jungle for a long and chastening walk home.

When the lawyers went on strike, made a ceremonial bonfire of their European clothes, and set up a charka - a spinning wheel, the symbol of the Congress party - in the bar library, I went along and asked them to give me spinning lessons; which, with some embarrassment but great good will, they consented to do.

When news of trouble at the Indian Iron and Steel Company's works was brought to us, Bill Cook, the policeman, and I were exercising our ponies on the polo ground. We rode straight from the ground to Hirapur, two miles away. The sudden appearance of two men on horseback, wielding long polo sticks, must have been a curious apparition to the rioters. We turned it into a game of hide and seek, giving them two minutes to make themselves scarce. Then, to the accompaniment of much laughter and shouting of slogans, in which we joined in, we rounded up the remnants, and shepherded them out of harm's way.

One Sunday afternoon we heard that several bus loads of hired thugs had been imported from neighbouring Bihar to make trouble at Kulti, where there was another large iron and steel works. Cook and I drove out together, ordering a posse of armed police to follow. When we arrived, about one hundred and fifty stalwarts were gathering on top of a rise, exhorting each other to mischief. They saw us and came streaming downhill towards us. We had outstripped the posse; but to retreat, or even to stand our ground, would have been unwise. We ran uphill to meet them, beckoning and shouting to non-existent reinforcements to follow. The mob hesitated, and then turned back, leaving one small boy piddling in our direction, a gallant gesture of defiance. We patted him on the head, and continued up the hill. By the time we reached the top we had been joined by our armed police, who surrounded the place, carefully leaving some escape routes open. We gave deliberately loud instructions about inspection of weapons and distribution of ammunition, and in five minutes the hilltop was deserted.

I exceeded my powers on several occasions. An important member of the Congress party visited the Sub-Division, bringing with him lantern slides to accompany a series of speeches. I doubted whether these would be innocuous lectures, and insisted on examining the slides. They proved to be, from the point of view of a conscientious sub-Divisional Officer, misleading and inflammatory propaganda. Instead of waiting to arrest the speaker after his mischief had been done, I seized the slides before he could give his lecture. He was a better lawyer than I was; he pointed out volubly that I had not been gazetted with the powers to do this - and he was right. My authority from the Government to do this arbitrary and unlawful deed followed a week later.

During a Muhammadan festival, when sparks could fly among the dynamite of political tension, I suggested to the local Commander of the Chota Nagpur Regiment, a volunteer Light Horse unit of which I was a member, that it might be a timely exercise to 'show the flag' with a route march through Asansol town. It seemed to me at the time a fairly harmless precaution, though a more mature reflection suggests that there was some risk of it being provocative. I heard later that I was about to be officially reprimanded for calling out the military in aid of the civil power, without the permission of government; but the Governor of Bengal, Sir Stanley Jackson - a famous cricketer of his time, who probably knew more about spin bowling than the niceties of administration - thought it had not been such a bad idea, and cancelled the reprimand.

I was rash and inexperienced, but we had little serious trouble in Asansol, and no terrorist crime. In Midnapore, another west Bengal district south of Asansol, it was a different story. There, three District Magistrates in succession were murdered, all in the space of a few months. The manner in which each of them met his death illustrates both the vulnerability of the administrator who will not be deterred from going about his business, and the determination of the assassins. One was shot while going round an exhibition of local crafts; another was shot in the back through an open window when seated at a District Board meeting, and the third as he walked on to the field to play in a football match, his bodyguards having accompanied him as far as the touch line.

After one of these murders it was reported that some of the terrorists responsible might be hiding in one or other of two houses in Asansol which were known to be headquarters of nationalist parties. It seemed to me unlikely that terrorists on the run would choose such known addresses as a hide-out, but Cook and I each took one of the houses for a midnight raid. Such operations are difficult to conduct secretly. The house is usually one of an inter-connected hive of dwellings in a congested bazaar, with many ways of escape over the roof tops, and almost impossible for a police party to surround completely and without being seen. I had no right to be acting as a policeman on this occasion, but there was no time to study the rule book. I left the disposition of his force to an Indian Police Inspector, but I had to be the first man in. I would not like to repeat the experience of that house-search at night, walking up a dark stair, revolver in one hand and an electric torch, held well away from me, in the other. I was afraid and I had to keep telling myself that the other man, if he was there, had more to be afraid of, since the odds were against him.

But it was an anti-climax, as most of such searches were. The bird, if there was one, had flown. All I found in the upper room was a stock of Gandhi caps, some seditious pamphlets and revolutionary badges made in Japan.

The only other manifestations of terrorism in Asansol were threatening messages, written in blood and thrown over my garden wall, and some home-made bombs, cigarette tins filled with explosive and steel gramophone needles, which fortunately were discovered by the police before they were exploded.

The expatriate community of Asansol were hard-working, hard drinking and racially mixed. There were Welsh and Scots colliery managers; there were British, Canadians and Americans engaged in steel manufacture; Greeks and Armenians in other forms of industry and commerce.

Most Europeans and all government officers went armed in those days, not that it would have availed much for self-protection, but it might have been a deterrent. The precaution was almost as dangerous as the cause that promoted it. One of my anxieties was the careless way in which some of my compatriots, after a few measures of Dutch courage, would brandish their weapons in the club bar. Later it became a convention to deposit arms in a convenient place, under guard, when we entered the club or a private house.

Station polo flourished in Asansol, and although not of a high standard, it was played with great enthusiasm. American and Armenian oaths mingled with honest Welsh and English. I acquired a middle-aged pony with beautiful manners, who had played in tournaments, and he proceeded to teach me the game. The S.D.O's bungalow - a condemned government building, the only one which still had pull-punkahs and oil lamps, in a town blazing with electricity and whirring with fans - had the advantage of being near the polo ground, so that I could practise to my heart's content.

The polo ground was also the parade ground of our local Light Horse Unit. I had joined this, enlisting my pony as a charger, in order to help pay for his keep. The parades were not always well attended, but as I lived next door, I could not default without a good excuse. Sometimes the Troop Commander and Corporal Brass - a neighbouring colliery manager, who wore British and French war medals (probably unauthorised) - and Trooper Christie were the only soldiers on parade. Corporal Brass would then be told to take Trooper Christie on a mounted reconnaissance, which he would enliven with tall stories of his wartime adventures in two armies, from both of which he claimed to have deserted, while our commanding officer read a several-months-old 'Tatler', on the club verandah.

Calcutta, one hundred and twenty miles away, was our metropolis and Mecca. There were bright lights and the fleshpots; theatres, concerts, Chowringhee, the Maidan and a wealth of fine eighteenth century houses: and there was the seat of government and the ladder of promotion. When, after nearly two years in Asansol, I was called to Calcutta to be an under-secretary in Writers' Buildings, I found the city beautiful and desirable. For me Calcutta still had the airs and graces of a grande dame: it took the war years to turn her into a drab.

Writers' Buildings was a sombre secretariat in Dalhousie Square, not far from the supposed site of the Black Hole. Its name gave it an aura of John Company's days, when young writers of the Honourable East India Company, 'griffins' like myself, would copy out in beautiful copper-plate the letters which might take six months, under sail, to reach their destination in the City of London.

In 1931 a political and social transition was taking place. Constitutionally, a dyarchy was operating, one of the planned stages on the road to self-government, under which some Indian Ministers, with responsibility for particular 'nation-building' subjects, were included in the Governor's Executive Council alongside official colleagues. Socially, the signs of prosperity and the extravagancies of the twenties were disappearing, as well as some of the mutual exclusiveness between the races. Europeans were mixing more freely with Indians, especially with the Brahmo Samaj families which predominated in the Bengali upper middle class of Calcutta. Edwardian conventions, such as stiff collars and the routine of calling cards, were dying, but dying hard. The clouds of economic depression were rolling in, and scarcely a week passed when the lightning of terrorism did not strike.

It was an exciting and stimulating time for a young man who was ready to burn the candle at both ends. Revolutionary violence was endemic in a small but fanatical minority of a people whose language and culture was different from that of the rest of India; who had an ancient grievance against authority, since the days of the Moguls; and who carried the stigma of an unmartial race. It fed on the resurgence of Asian nationalism after the Japanese victories over the Russians at the beginning of the century, was fanned by the discontents flowing from the first partition of Bengal, and later from the liberal and methodical steps towards self-government to which the British rulers were already committed, and which therefore gave the movement the colour of a war of independence.

There had been isolated incidents of terrorist violence over a number of years: what caused the flare-up in the early thirties was probably the increasing rivalry between the two Bengali revolutionary parties, whose acquaintance I had already made, physically and symbolically, on the football ground at Mymensingh. That rivalry was also the inherent weakness of the movement.

It seemed anything but weak at the time. These were the days of the Chittagong Armoury raid, the raid on Writers' Buildings and on the Railway Institute at Chittagong. Judges were shot dead in court; district magistrates and police officers, British and Indian, were killed, blinded or maimed. A bomb was thrown at Sir Charles Tegart, Commissioner of Police, in Dalhousie Square. There was an attempt on the life of the Governor, Sir Stanley Jackson, while he was addressing the Calcutta University Convocation; on his successor, Sir John Anderson, at the Lebong racecourse, near Darjeeling; and on the leader of the European parliamentry group in his Calcutta office. The vulnerability of the targets was increased by the determination that normal life and business should go on as usual.

A feature of the violence was the number of young women involved. C.G.B. Stevens, an outstanding district officer, beloved of many Bengalis, was shot dead outside his house in Comilla by two schoolgirls while he was reading a petition which they had presented. Another feature was the suicidal desperation of some of the assassins, who carried packets of cyanide which they swallowed when the deed was done.

Whatever he may think of himself, or other Indians may think of him, the Bengali is not a coward. His bravery, when occasion demands, is the more remarkable because he is by nature pacific. I remember particularly police sub-inspectors and subordinate civil officers in remote stations, usually unarmed, whose loyalty and courage in those dark days were of a very high order.

Bengalis could be foolhardy as well as brave. I was driving with a colleague along a street in Dacca which had an unhealthy reputation, when a young Bengali ran from the side of the road and jumped on the running-board of our car. There was a moment of uncertainty, but he turned out to be a plainclothes policeman, determined to protect us, in the course of duty, from possible assassins. He was lucky not to have received two bullets in his own body before he had explained his appearance in our midst.

Sir John Anderson - whose name later became associated with air-raid shelters in Britain - came out in 1932 to be Governor of Bengal, with the reputation of an Under-Secretary of State in the Home Office whose methodical efficiency had helped to restore law and order, temporarily, in Ireland.

Gradually terrorism in Bengal was brought under control, but the price had been heavy. Wounded men had died in distant places because of the delay in bringing medical aid to them. One of my tasks was to arrange the purchase of an amphibious aeroplane, able to alight on and take off from the rivers of East Bengal, which became vast inland seas in the monsoon. It was a good insurance policy. By the time the aeroplane was delivered, we were over the hump of our troubles, and it never had to be used for a victim of terrorists, though its worth was proved in other errands of mercy.

The Auxillary Force in India, like the territorials, provided an opportunity for peacetime military training combined with social exercise. For some reason young officials were not encouraged to join, but in Asansol I had not asked anyone's permission to join the Chota Nagpur Light Horse, and had nearly been carpeted for my association with it. I therefore had not much hope of being allowed to join the Calcutta Light Horse but my Chief Secretary was a keen horseman, and was persuaded to make an exception in my case. In this way I got to know many men of my own age in the merchant community, and to hear their sometimes abrasive opinions of the Government and its policies -

a salutary experience for a young white brahmin.

Our parades in Calcutta were taken more seriously than those of the Chota Nagpur Regiment, and our annual camps in the Santhal Pergannahs of Behar were a combination of energetic soldiering and riotous night life. The riding school was a stern test, and those who came through it were horsemen. Many of the chargers were mettlesome steeds which competed at Tollygunge races under their 'gentlemen rider' owners when off duty. Their sternest test was the Proclamation Day Parade on New Year's Day every year - to commemorate Queen Victoria's proclamation as Empress of India - when the Cossipore Artillery drawn up immediately on our right boomed out a salute, and the ranks of the Light Horse would sway like a cornfield in a breeze.

The main attraction of the Calcutta Light Horse for me was the opportunity it gave for playing polo, a game to which I had become addicted in Asansol; and my earlier experience enabled me to qualify for the regimental team in the Christmas tournaments. I had to ride strange ponies for I could not afford to keep more than one who had taught me the game, and he was by now rather slow for tournament polo. That was a handicap when drawn against better-mounted teams fielded by regular cavalry regiments or Indian princes. I remember, in a match against Darbhanga, racing the young maharajah for the ball: he came up from behind and passed me, but turned with exquisite politeness to say 'sorry!' before he struck the ball away.

There were mounted paper-chases and morning exercise on the race-course, half enveloped in a layer of river mist, so that one had the illusion of a number of disembodied heads bobbing about on top of it, and gravely saluting each other as they passed. There was rugby football in the rains, and swimming at the Saturday Club - all of which gave me a good appetite; I shudder now to think of the breakfasts I ate when I returned from exercise to the United Service Club, and which caused older members to remark, screwing monocles into their eyes, 'My God! You must be feeling healthy.'

There followed long days in office, and the decoding of cypher telegrams late into the night. It was a curious mixture of a life; clouded by the grim reality of an emergency, but with cheerfulness continually breaking through.

Indeed there was more than cheerfulness, for after some light-hearted adventures I found myself deeply and irrevocably in love with the girl who was to share the next twenty-six years of my life in India. She had come with what had been rudely known, since the days of William Hickey, as the 'fishing fleet'; daughters brought out by their parents for a winter season in Calcutta. Never had the cargo of any fleet surpassed in loveliness that of 1932. It was as if Ulysses himself had netted all the sirens in the Tyrrhenian Sea, and sailed with them to India.

Calculating mamas used to tell their daughters that an I.C.S. husband was worth four hundred pounds a year, alive or dead, referring to the widow's pension of those days. The girls of 1932 were not calculating, nor, even if they had wished to go fishing, would they have had room to cast their nets - the crowd around them was so thick, and the competition so fierce.

Their arrival wrought a magic transformation in us. Hard-riding, boot-slapping clodhoppers became overnight polished performers of the dance floor. Breakfast parties at the Tollygunje Club, after quiet hacks through the jungle, moonlight picnics by the Dhakuria Lake or in Barrackpore Park, became the order of the day and night. Somehow the working day had to be fitted in as well, so that there was little time to sleep.

The social round in Calcutta included a good deal of ceremonial and, as it were, official-social occasions, which involved hard work for under-secretaries, and dressing up in hot political uniform. There were the arrivals and departures of Viceroys and other visiting potentates; balls and garden parties at Government House and at Belvedere, the viceregal palace in Alipore. There were Durbars, at which the Governor conferred the insignia of honours on behalf of the King-Emperor, and the Political Under-Secretary, perspiring freely would march and counter-march for hours to present the recipients. Thereafter he had to distribute among them His Imperial Majesty's hospitality in the form of betel-nut wrapped in pan leaf wrapped in gold or silver foil, according to the rank of the recipient, and a drop of attar of roses for each, which caused the under-secretary himself to smell sweet for several days.

When, in April, the hot weather set in, making Calcutta barely tolerable, and again later, between the monsoon and the winter, the senior ranks of Government, with a reduced staff, would make their way up the Himalayan foot hills to Darjeeling. Under-secretaries left behind in Calcutta could relax sartorially, though not in their labours, which the split personality of the Government tended to increase. Sometimes they were lucky and were summoned up to the heights for a spell. Then did one realise how keen are the pleasures of contrast. We gulped down the cool, clean air like champagne, and felt new men within the hour; and right in front of us, when the clouds lifted, was the superb vision of snow-mantled

Kanchenjunga. Every moment was precious. Sleep was an unnecessary encumbrance: who needed it? Few though we were, the younger generation must have been a sore trial to their tolerant seniors, for the Darjeeling Club, the Chowrastha and the Planters' Quarterdeck seemed to be full of young men and women looking for candles with two ends to burn.

My appointment was drawing to an end, and the time had come when I must, once more, take leave temporarily of my heart.

> Gladly, ere night had left the skies
> My love and I would go,
> To watch with wonder in our eyes
> Dawn's crimson flood the snow.
> And there we found a shining thing;
> We found a rainbow for our ring.

My Muse, five years older, was at it again. There is some poetic license in the description of what happened, but it was a fitting end to a period.

At four o'clock one morning we mounted our ponies and, in pouring rain, rode to the top of Tiger Hill. A few feet below the summit we came out of the cloud, and there, spread beneath us was a woolly, white sheet stretching all the way to the foot of Kanchenjunga. But our eyes were fixed on a small point, far distant. The light changed from grey to paler grey; and suddenly, as we watched, the small point glowed like a ruby: Everest, the pinnacle of the world.

Minutes later the sun rose, and as we turned to go, we looked down at the cloud. The Brocken Spectre had caught us. Our gigantic shadows were thrown onto the white sheet, and round them was the unbroken circle of a rainbow. It was a moment of great promise.

4

Hill Tracts

When my wife Elizabeth and I, dusty after two days of travelling across India, stepped out of the mail train onto the platform of Howrah station, Calcutta's western rail terminus, we were greeted by Dasrath Mahakur, our Oriya bearer. Dasrath had been personal servant to a succession of I.C.S. officers, for long periods in each case, and he was getting on in years. With one exception he had never served, as it were, outside the Service. That exception was his very first employment, when he had come up to Calcutta as a boy from his village in Orissa, and had been engaged by an Australian jockey. He did not like talking about that experience, and we could only guess at the reason; but I suspect that he felt it had been a youthful indiscretion, beneath his dignity, and somehow a blot on his service record.

He seemed to be related to most of the other Oriya bearers in Calcutta, all of whom came from a small group of villages in Orissa which produced the finest bearers in India. The name derives, according to some pundits, from 'behara', and from a time when Bihar and Orissa were a single outlying appendage of Bengal. They were a professional caste who took great pride in their work, were scrupulously honest, utterly reliable and uncompromisingly loyal. They were important people in our lives, for on them depended in large measure our comfort, wellbeing and peace of mind in circumstances which were not always easy.

Their standards were sometimes irksome to twentieth century employers, for they had been inherited from days when their masters expected to be shaved in bed without being woken, then bathed, dried and encased from head to foot in the appropriate clothing for the day. I had made it clear to Dasrath that I required none of these attentions, but it took some time to wean him from the last vestigial remnant of his professional privileges, which was to seize me by the feet as I came out of the bathroom and attempt to dry between my toes.

Dasrath had become used, before I met him, to being a family bearer: he got on well with memsahibs, and liked to have fair-haired children tugging at his dhoti and prattling the bad

Bengali and worse Hindustani which they picked up from him. He was, in fact, rather an old woman, and had only suffered me in my bachelor days in the impatient expectation that I would in due course acquire a wife.

He was, however, - and it was one of his great merits - a mine of information. He knew all the service gossip and, although he would not admit it, probably all the scandal too. It was never necessary to warn him of the date and time when we should be returning from leave - he was always on the station platform to meet us. My first question, therefore, was: 'Well, Dasrath, where have we been posted? No one has told me yet.'

'I heard that Huzoor (the Presence) was first posted as Additional District Magistrate of Midnapore; but in the last few days this has been changed, and the Presence is now posted as Deputy Commissioner of the Chittagong Hill Tracts. This is, no doubt, an honour; and in due course the Sahib will surely become a Lord Sahib. But it is a bad district, unhealthy and very far away. You have ten days joining time, so that there is still an opportunity to petition the Chief Secretary, and have the posting changed.'

Poor Dasrath; it would indeed be exile for him, but I was delighted with the news. I had no right to expect, after less than six years service, a district charge of my own.

And what a district! The Chittagong Hill Tracts, now the eastern-most district of Bangladesh, is a strip about forty miles wide and one hundred and fifty miles long, running roughly north and south, parallel to the coast of the Bay of Bengal and beginning twenty miles inland from Chittagong, the coastal district which takes its name from the port at the mouth of the Karnaphuli river. Throughout the length of the Chittagong Hill Tracts run parallel spines, low foot-hills two or three hundred feet high along the district boundary, rising in corrugations towards the east up to ridges of three or four thousand feet along the Assam and Burma borders.

Through the valleys flow the main rivers, the Karnaphuli, the Sangu, the Matamuri, fed by innumerable tributaries and streams which rise in almost impenetrable head-water forest reserves, or in the highlands of Hill Tipperah, the Lushai Hills of Assam and the Arakan Hills of Burma. They are small rivers by Bengal standards, full of rapids in the upper reaches and sand bars lower down, and although they are not easy to navigate they provide, since roads are few and very far between, the most convenient means of communication for the traveller. I do not expect that has changed much in fifty years.

The hills are covered with many varieties of bamboo, some as thin as a man's finger, some as thick as a flagstaff, fifty feet high and over-arching, so that one can walk by elephant tracks through a bamboo forest for days and hardly see the sun.

Where the bamboo has been cut and burnt on the hillsides for the shifting cultivation known as 'jhuming', a prolific blue-flowered shrub, a kind of ageratum, takes its place until the bamboo is regenerated; and this, when it blooms, gives a smoky blue character to the more open valleys and slopes. It is a beautiful but ominous colour, for the soil is never so fertile where ageratum or coarse elephant grass grows, as under good bamboo ashes.

There is little flat land, and that mostly along the lower reaches of the rivers and their tributaries. This had been settled under plough cultivation, and the tenants were mainly Chakmas, the most sophisticated of the dozen or so tribes which inhabit the district. Some of them had sub-let their land to immigrant Bengali Muslims from Chittagong.

Into this narrow strip of territory a mixture of cheerful, easy-going, and, on the whole, law-abiding highlanders had been driven over the centuries by the pressure of more vigorous neighbours, or perhaps at the end of migration they had come to rest in the last hills before the coastal plain. They shared, in varying degrees, the culture known as Indonesian, which is found throughout Asia from Assam to Borneo, and they had a generally Mongolian appearance; but there were marked differences between them in customs, dress (or the lack of it) and in speech, and they were exclusive, self-contained communities, divided as much in their preferences whether for living on hill-tops or on river banks, as by the narrow valleys and the dense jungle.

Each village or group of jhum houses had its headman, chosen by the villagers but appointed by authority – a kind of arbiter of custom and collector of dues: and there were three Chiefs of the three main tribal divisions; the Bohmong Chief in the south, whose mixed assortment of adherents, including Moghs, Mrungs, Mrus and Khumis, were distantly related to the Arakan Burmese; the Chakma Chief in the middle, whose people had mingled with the plainsmen and aped the dress and speech of Bengalis; and the Mong Chief, or Rani – for she was a woman in my time – to whom a loosely-knit collection of Tippera clans owed an ill-defined allegiance.

The chiefs, whose forbears had been leading tribesmen chosen by the Government to be tax-collectors, still exercised a restricted tribal authority which, naturally enough, they were continually trying to enlarge. This sometimes came into conflict with the overall responsibilities of the Deputy Commissioner, who had to be vigilant for unauthorised exactions and petty tyrannies. I was to have much to do with the Chiefs while I was in the Hill Tracts, and I like to think that we

Kuki girl, Saichal Ridge

Mrung dancers

remained friends. I got on especially well with Bohmongri Kyaw Jaw Sainfru Chowdry, an old rascal with a pink silk headscarf, ceremonial umbrella, a strong head for whisky and the manners of a dandy from Rangoon. But the warmth of our mutual feelings was always tempered with wariness.

It was towards this exciting territory that we were bound, when the Deputy Commissioner's small launch 'Pioneer' caught the tide one morning at Chittagong to carry us up the Karnaphuli River to Rangamati, headquarters of the district - my wife, myself and Dasrath Mahakur, by now resigned to his fate.

The Karnaphuli was to figure largely in our lives, as it was the first link in our slender chain of communication with the outside world. Whether towards the comparative civilisation of the coast, or towards the mountains and forests in the north and east, most journeys from Rangamati began on that river, first by launch, as far as launches could go, then by flat-bottomed country boat, then by dug-out canoe and finally by elephant or on foot. In some directions the tracks and fragile wooden or bamboo bridges would allow a bicycle to be used for a few miles. There were no motorable roads in the Hill Tracts in those days - a fact which, paradoxically, increased the efficiency of the touring officer - and horses, according to veterinary advice, could not survive there. No one, before the war, had thought of mules for travelling in those hills.

Karnaphuli means the flower - or jewel - in the ear. We thought it an uninteresting tidal river for the first twelve miles or so from Chittagong, but signs of the hill tracts soon began to meet us: country boats with round matting roofs; sampans gaily painted with an eye on each side of the bow and scorpion-tailed sterns, laden with baskets of the short-staple cotton that grows in the jhums; and enormous rafts of bamboos drifting down from the forest reserves. Then an outline of low hills appeared on the horizon, and as the river turned towards them, we drew in the bank to make my first call inside my new district.

It was the Baptist Mission hospital at Chandraghona, in the charge of a German medical missionary, Dr. G.O. Teichmann. He had worked at Chandraghona for many years with his wife, two nurses, an able assistant and a bare minimum of equipment. There were few modern conveniences at Chandraghona, not even electricity; but that was of no concern to the crowds frequenting Dr. Teichmann's hospital, for he had acquired a legendary reputation as an expert in the treatment of malarial fevers, of which the hill tracts contained an ample assortment. He did not claim to be a specialist in leprosy, but a leper colony had established itself near the hospital. He taught the lepers how to treat themselves and each other, and instructed them in crafts, carpentry, house-building and husbandry. They in turn taught the new arrivals, for he turned none away. He did not try to proselytize his patients, but many of them became Christians. He was the best kind of missionary.

Dr. Teichmann gave us good advice. We were entering an unhealthy district where malignant tertian and blackwater fever were rife. My Bengali predecessor had been carried out on a stretcher with cerebral malaria. Dr. Teichmann's theory was that some of the aggravated forms, and especially blackwater fever, were caused by their suppression in earlier stages through regular doses of quinine. This was before the days of more sophisticated anti-malarial drugs.

'I expect you have been told to take quinine every day' he said. 'Don't do it: If you get wet through or exhausted, and your resistance is lowered, take a large dose, but make it the exception, not the rule.'

We took his advice, and, although we were not entirely free from other ills, Elizabeth and I both escaped malaria, almost miraculously, in the hill tracts and for ever after.

We continued our journey as the narrowing river wound through the hills and began to earn its lovely name. We avoided rocks, skirted whirl-pools, slithered over sand banks, and at last, after ten hours against the stream, we arrived at Rangamati. A public launch service from Chittagong, with passengers, mail and stores, used to make the journey every day, except for interruptions of a week or more when the river was in spate, and took twelve or more hours upstream and six or seven down. It became an important time-table for us.

Rangamati used to occupy a long, narrow shoulder of the hills, at the upper end of which stood the Forest Officer's house and the Police Lines, and at the lower end, the District Hospital and the bazaar. Also on the lower level was a small open space surrounded by magnificent mahogany trees which were festooned with orchids, yellow and mauve in their season. This space served as parade ground, park, promenade and general place of public recreation. Between the upper and the lower level, on progressively rising ground, were the kutcherry, that is court house and government offices, the Deputy Commissioner's bungalow, the Circuit House, for visiting senior officers, a small club house, a missionary's house (seldom occupied) and the High School for boys and girls. That was all. The shoulder formed a peninsula round which the Karnaphuli flowed in a hairpin bend.

I say 'used to occupy' because the lower end of the peninsula, with the mahogany trees, is now submerged beneath a lake which covers most of the Karnaphuli valley, formed by the dam for a hydro-electric scheme which the Pakistan government built some miles above Chandraghona. The water now laps the walls of the kutcherry, a massive loop-holed building, which was originally a fort. The D.C's terraced garden which, when I knew it, stood a clear two hundred feet above the river, is now reduced to a few shrubs round a landing stage.

When we stepped ashore we had a stiff climb to our new abode. It was an old single-storeyed house, with a thatched roof, walls of bamboo matting covered by plaster, and cement floors, except in the large round central drawing room, which had an uneven wooden floor. The living rooms, behind a deep verandah, were generously supplied with doors and windows, open - except during the monsoon - to every breeze that blew, and fortunately so, for the house was only a few feet above sea level, and had not the benefit of electric fans. In front there projected a covered patio, like the bridge of a ship, with a magnificent view across the river and open valley to range after range of distant hills.

From the roof of the patio fell a cascade of flaming bignonia creeper. The garden, at various levels, was full of flowering and fruit trees - mango and leechees, grevillea, a rare amherstia and clumps of bamboo. On a space at the back of the house was the ruin of a cement tennis court. There were no flower beds and few shrubs, until Elizabeth introduced them later; but we woke one morning, after a spring rain-storm, to find that the paths and terraces had exploded into a profusion of amaryllis lilies, white, scarlet and parti-coloured hybrids.

At the bottom of the garden, some way from the servants' quarters, was an out-house, which had been used by my predecessor as a private zoo, and before that, I gathered, as a bibi-khana, where some earlier, lonely deputy commissioner had kept his concubines. In its recesses I unearthed a round wooden table-top which, when cleaned and polished, revealed a number of carved initials and regimental crests. Clearly it had been a mess table for officers engaged in the various expeditions into the Chin Hills and Lushai Hills to repel marauders into the settled district of Chittagong, military operations of long ago for which Rangamati had been the base.

This outwardly desirable residence had one drawback. It was haunted. It was Dasrath Mahakur, of course, who first discovered the story, and came to tell me about it, with his eyes popping out of his head. It was the ghost, he said of a woman who had either committed suicide or had been murdered by her husband in our bedroom. I suspected that this might be a last, desperate effort by Dasrath to dislodge us from the place of exile. I forbad him to breathe a word about it to my wife, and made light of the story.

But it was not to be laughed off so easily. One night I

woke to hear a gentle, regular tapping on the wooden slats of the bedroom door onto the verandah. Elizabeth had heard it too. At first I thought it was the nightwatchman; then I remembered that we had dispensed with him, and there was a police sentry at the other side of the house. I called out; there was no answer, but the tapping stopped. Then it started again. I got up and looked in the verandah: there was nothing there. I asked the sentry, but he had seen and heard nothing. I told him to verify that all the servants were in their quarters, but not to call them out. He reported that they were all at home, and apparently asleep. I went back to bed. The tapping began again, a soft persistent rhythm, as if someone wanted to come in. It was unnerving. We decided to move to another room, but did not get much sleep that night.

In the cold light of morning, I tried to persuade myself that it had only been a dog scratching itself against the door- but it was not a convincing explanation. Secretly ashamed of admitting the possibility of a supernatural cause, I begged the spirit to be at rest and not trouble us, for we were kindly disposed. I trust that this message was received, in whatever is the abode of restless spirits, as a prayer. At any rate, the prayer seemed to be answered for we heard no more tapping, and after a few nights plucked up courage to return to our bedroom.

The Chittagong Hill Tracts was a non-regulation district; that is to say it was administered under a special statute, and was not subject to the codes and procedures of the rest of Bengal. The Deputy Commissioner was answerable to the Commissioner in Chittagong, and through him to the Board of Revenue in Calcutta; but these authorities were far away and were infrequent visitors. A shoe-string administration, stripped to its essentials, simple and personal, was considered best for such a district. Responsibilities which were normally distributed among a number of executives were therefore concentrated on the shoulders of one man. No one, except Pooh Bah, has ever been such a compendium of officialdom as the Deputy Commissioner of the Chittagong Hill Tracts.

Not only was I the Deputy Commissioner, I was also Superintendent of Police and District Judge - the latter for civil cases only, for although the convention of separating executive from judiciary was largely ignored in Rangamati (without any obvious injustice), the line had to be drawn somewhere; and it was drawn at Sessions Judge, the higher court for criminal prosecutions. That function was reserved for the Commissioner, for any serious criminals in the Hill Tracts might reasonably feel that the dice were loaded against them if they were liable to be arrested, committed for trial and tried by one and the same person. I was District Engineer (Public Works

Department), Inspector of Schools, Public Health Officer and District Agricultural Officer, and I spent much of my time writing letters to myself and going to another office to answer them. The only official posts I did not hold were those of Civil Surgeon, Forest Officer and Postmaster. This economical arrangement considerably reduced the number of officials usually to be found at a district headquarters.

The Civil Surgeon was a querulous Bengali who believed that he had been banished to a penal settlement through the machination of enemies. The real reason was more likely to have been his utter incompetence. He once had to give me an anti-tetanus injection, whereupon I swelled up like a balloon, developed a high fever and had to be shipped down to Chittagong, where the Irish Civil Surgeon put me right with two shots of adrenalin, muttering something uncomplimentary about his colleague. We thanked our lucky stars that Dr. Teichmann was within reach in an emergency.

The only European officials in the district beside ourselves were the Forest Officer and his wife, and an officer of the Survey of India, seconded from the Royal Engineers and engaged at the time in scientifically mapping the hill tracts. The existing maps had been drawn apparently in free-hand at the end of the last century by optimists who had climbed to a vantage point and sketched in, by guesswork, the lie of the jungle, the course of the streams and the position of hidden, movable villages. There were also a missionary and his wife – in addition to the mission hospital at Chandraghona – who had a house in Rangamati, but were seldom at home, for they administered a few schools in remote valleys with the help of two devoted young women. These we hardly ever saw, and their tongue-tied embarrassment when they met their own kind and tried to speak their own language was painful to behold.

The company of these people was the more precious because it was rare. We – all three senior officers – shared the only two launches, the tiny 'Pioneer' and the even smaller 'Baby', so that when one officer was at headquarters, the others were usually out on tour. There was a miniature Club, whose membership consisted mainly of Bengali clerks and officials. It had just enough room for a badminton court and a bridge four – the most communal bridge I have ever seen, for all the members present would gather round, comment aloud on the contents of each hand and offer noisy advice on the playing of it.

We did not lack other forms of companionship. Visitors, usually in parties, dressed in all sorts of finery, would arrive at the D.C.'s bungalow from distant corners of the district, settle themselves on the verandah and smoke, cough and chatter until they could be seen. It was a convention that they should

have a preliminary discussion of their business with the D.C.
personally before proceeding to the kutcherry for more formal
disposal of the matter. It might be a question of jhum tax, a
gun license, the iniquities of Bengali traders, a complaint
against the Chief or tales of crop damage by elephants; or it
might be to hear the latest news, or a courtesy visit, or just
to pass the time. They would often bring gifts, a basket of
eggs or fruit, sometimes an animal. We soon acquired a
slow-loris - a nocturnal, sloth-like animal - and a spotted fawn
which had been found motherless in the jungle. Elizabeth fed it
on milk off her finger-tips and it followed her everywhere,
butting her angrily in the calf at meal-time. After some weeks
it caught cold and died, the first sadness in our married life.
We soon had to decline gifts of live animals, or our house would
have become a menagerie. This did not avoid the occasional
offering of a stuffed tiger or leopard, which had been ringed
and killed by villagers with spears, for there was a price on
the head of these marauders.

There was plenty of work. After I had counted the rupees,
the stamps and the opium in the Treasury on my first day, I
sampled the work in court. Lawyers were not allowed to practise
in the Hill Tracts; the parties had to plead their own cases
and the magistrate had to conduct his own examination - and
probably got nearer to the heart of the matter in that way,
although language presented a difficulty. There were so many
dialects spoken in the district that, although I could speak
Bengali and soon picked up some Chakma and Moghi, I still had
often to use an interpreter, sometimes two.

I was tempted to hold court on the verandah of my house, as
one of my predecessors used to do, sitting in a tin bath tub up
to his neck in water. The same man taught his cook, his bearer
and a chaprassie - a court messenger - to play bridge, in order
to recover from the cook (he said) a part of what he lost on the
bazaar bills.

I could not afford to spend much time in court at
headquarters, since I must get to know my district as soon as
possible, and the pace of touring would be slow. I decided that
the cases which arose near Rangamati involved either Bengalis or
the more bengalicised Chakmas, I could well leave these to my
efficient Bengali deputy magistrate, and would try other cases
on tour in the villages, where there was much work of other
kinds to be done.

There appeared to be three tasks in particular which should
have priority: the development of services in the district
generally, and especially of communications; the collection of
revenue, which was badly in arrears; and the discipline of the
Chittagong Hill Tracts Armed Police.

For development we made a three-year plan. The Bengal Government was in a generous mood, and grants were available for rural development, if the villagers themselves would contribute part of the cost in money or labour. I was determined that the Hill Tracts should get their fair share, - if not more - of the allocations. The single-minded co-operation of the various departments, which composed me, and a new-found energy among the hillmen (once they were persuaded to look upon it as a game designed to extract money out of the Government) were able, between them to accomplish much. Before long, many miles of road were added or widened, bridges were built, tanks dug, wells sunk, new schools and dispensaries were set up. In Rangamati itself the first electricity appeared, enough to light the main street, and to pump water from the river and distribute it, filtered, through the bazaar.

The revenue collection played its part. My predecessor had been a sick man and unable to tour regularly, so that government dues had not been collected for nearly two years. They were of two kinds, jhum tax and plough rent. The jhum tax was assessed on each of those households which practised an ancient, primitive form of cultivation, moving about the hills and never settling in one place for more than four or five years. The jhumias cut and burned the bamboo or other jungle in a patch on the hillside and, when the first rains moistened the ashes and the soil, they would dig holes and throw into them handfuls of mixed seed, of cotton, paddy, millet, maize and of the red or yellow coxcomb flower. These, as they emerged in turn, gave the household a cash crop, grain for food and for beer, and some colour to decorate their bamboo dwellings built on stilts. The plough rent was assessed by area on the few settled lowland farmers. Both taxes were simple and light; but no one will go out of his way to pay a tax: I saw that, in order to overcome the inertia after two years tax holiday, I should have to go out and collect it myself, and, to sweeten the pill, must provide some attraction, turning each collection into a gala day. Sometimes it was the police band, often it was the police elephants, but, most successful of all, was the Deputy Commissioner's wife who, dressed in khaki shirt, shorts and topi, could easily be and often was mistaken for the Deputy Commissioner himself. There were occasions when the enthusiasm for this exhibit was such, when her real identity had been established, that I had to draw a circle round her in the dust and say 'Thus far and no further', to inquisitive village women who had never seen a memsahib before, and were intent on exploring if she were white all through. The entertainment was worth paying for: the money came rolling in, and no government could deny development grants to a district which paid up even its arrears of revenue with such a good grace.

Police discipline was a tougher nut to crack. The civil police were no problem, but there was a company of Armed Police, a relic of more disturbed times and of those long-forgotten military expeditions into the hills beyond. Now they had nothing to do, which was demoralising, and discipline was bad. Nearly all were heavily in debt to local shopkeepers, and they drank a good deal more country spirit than was good for them. Gradually the debts were cleared, and a controlled canteen and shop were set up in the police lines.

I sent parties away on physical training courses, and others to learn to play the bagpipes and drums with the Eastern Frontier Rifles at Dacca. Eventually our band was almost as large as the rest of the force, and they were justly proud of it. I gave them new uniforms, and took them out on long route marches to sweat the vice out of them. Sometimes, on these marches, we varied the monotony with a field day, simple battle drill, with blank ammunition. I would point out a hill-top, and tell them we would take it, with sections advancing under covering fire. This tactic, however, soon had to be abandoned. Once I failed to notice, until I had led them into it, a small village hidden in the trees at the top of the hill; and such was the enthusiasm of my troops that they captured it with loud yells, chasing and unoffending villagers at bayonet point down the other side and into the jungle, from which they dared not emerge for several days.

I had two elephants on the police strength, Lal Bahadur, a fine young tusker, of whom more anon, and a middle-aged lady called Daisy who was said to be over fifty years old. She was young in spirit, however, for a few months before we arrived in Rangamati, she had wandered into the jungle and had an affair with a wild elephant, and so was on maternity leave for a long spell. After her calf was born - Marina, beause born on Princess Marina's wedding day - Daisy was no longer fit for police duty. I asked Government to sanction her a pension of six seers of paddy a day, and turned her loose in a forest reserve, near a Forest Department outpost. Every evening she would come out of the forest and eat her pension, at the end of a line of Forest Department elephants. For all I know she, or her descendants are doing it still.

The elephants are useful touring companions, usually as baggage carriers, but sometimes, in the early days, Elizabeth would climb onto Daisy or Lal Bahadur, and go on ahead of the slower, continually interrupted, pedestrian progress of the Deputy Commissioner-cum-Police Superintendent and his entourage for the stage of that day's march. Occasionally she would bicycle, with an orderly, through miles of elephant grass or jungle, and was lucky if she found rickety plank bridges over the streams, or a fordable crossing that did not involve total immersion; or she would travel by the various forms of river craft. Invariably she had to sleep rough. Sometimes we could pitch a tent or halt at a rest house, but more often our touring nights were spent in a hastily built bamboo basha or on the bottom of a dug-out canoe. So, what might have been a dull routine elsewhere was enlivened by a spice of adventure: but adventure is always pleasanter in retrospect. It was a hard, lonely and anxious life for a young wife with a family on the way, whose husband was absorbed in his new duties and for whom ordinary social contacts were practically non-existent. _Si jeunesse savait_ ---.

If we needed any compensation for the lack of civilised comforts, we had a material one - a good Mugh cook. The Mughs (related to but distinct from the Moghs) are the finest cooks in India. Even the Viceroy's household in far-off Delhi was never without a Mugh or two. They are Bengali Buddhists who come from a small group of villages near Chittagong. A close professional community, they are secretive about their recipes, and club together to send promising young Mughs abroad, to learn their craft and gather secrets in the kitchens of famous chefs in Paris and London.

Our Barua could have earned many times the salary we could afford to pay him, but once we had reached an understanding with him about the tolerable size of his bazaar bills (including concealed and unadmitted commissions), he decided that he liked us, and remained loyally with us for the rest of his days. In the Hill Tracts he would tour with us. He disliked walking, but must have found cycling along the winding paths through the hills almost as tedious, because he never learned either to dismount or to turn corners; the only way he could do so was to fall off and remount. At the end of the day's stage he would build his stove of three bricks and some mud, and turn out a three-course dinner which would have graced the Ritz.

Once, far out in the jungle, I saw that he had fever, and ordered him to bed. He fought to get up: "What will you eat?" he said, "You must not starve".

"I shall open a tin; what do you think I have brought them for? they are getting heavy to carry".

"It will be a great shame to me if you open a tin." He had to swallow the shame, and some aspirin and quinine too, but it was days before he forgave us.

We occasionally had visitors from outside the district. The Commissioner from Chittagong - I experienced five of them in succession - would come up the river every six months or so; but more often he decided, rightly, that it would be better for us, and preserve us from going 'jungly' (reverting to nature) if we were summoned down to Chittagong from time to time. One hard-drinking Commissioner who visited us brought with him a harder-drinking officer of the Eastern Frontier Rifles. Their visit coincided with heavy rain and a spate in the river, which tied them to Rangamati for longer than they had intended. My fairly ample stock of whisky began to sink at an alarming rate, and I was beginning to wonder if it would be proper for me to offer them country spirit - which is an aquired taste - when they decided to make a dash for it. I was rather relieved as I waved them good-bye from the landing stage: and the words were hardly out of my mouth when I saw the Commissioner's launch do a skid turn round the first bend of the river. I heard that the return journey to Chittagong was completed in record time.

The Board of Revenue, our masters in Calcutta, sometimes turned their thoughts in our direction. The Member-in-charge was Sir Brojendrs Lal Mitter, a charming, elderly Bengali lawyer. Urban Bengalis do not usually appreciate the backwoods, but Sir B.L. was an exception; he discovered that the Hill Tracts were his spiritual home, and he and his wife visited us more than once, bringing with them shrubs and tools for Elizabeth's garden, and pounds of tobacco for my pipe.

He insisted on exploring the jungles on an elephant while his Secretary and I took a short cut over the hills to meet him at some distant point for lunch. The Secretary was a Celt from the Western Isles, who recited long passages of Ossian to beguile the way; but when the Honourable Member was two hours overdue, we began to be anxious, and to wonder how and when we should officially announce his disappearance. But he turned up, late in the afternoon, full of enthusiasm for the intelligence of his elephant, who had refused to cross a stream at the point his mahout had indicated, and with great deliberation had chosen another crossing, more to his liking, several miles away.

Our most important visitor came in 1935, when we had been in the Hill Tracts for just over a year. He was the Governor of Bengal, Sir John Anderson - the same who, was Home Secretary in Winston Churchill's war-time Cabinet, and later became Lord Waverley. No Governor had visited Chittagong Hill Tracts in living memory, and Sir John said that he proposed to make an extended visit of ten days, with his complete staff and their wives, his sister and his daughter and a retinue of about a hundred persons. It was a great honour, but also a severe strain on the resources of a poor district and an unusual load of responsibility on its multi-purpose Deputy Commissioner.

I had a nightmare about this visit, that I should somehow be late for the Governor's arrival in my district. It was one of those terrible nightmares that come true.

The Durbar at Rangamati, 1935, Sir John Anderson's visit

Lal Bahadur carrying Sir John Anderson

The launches bringing the party were due to arrive in the
early afternoon at Kaptai, a small forest settlement beside the
river, where the hydro-electric dam has since been built. The
Forest Officer and I had been there since dawn, and had gone for
a walk to inspect the path along which we proposed to take His
Excellency that evening, as he was a keen forester and botanist
among other accomplishments. We returned before noon and, as we
reached the river bank, saw to our horror that the visiting
fleet had already moored alongside. The Governor had decided,
without warning us, to leave Chittagong earlier than had been
planned. No doubt security had something to do with it, for
terrorism was still a hazard in Bengal, and Sir John Anderson
had already been a target: all the more important was it that
from the moment the Governor set foot in my district until he
left, I should have been in a position to guard his person. I
felt as ashamed as if I had deserted my post, but H.E. did not
seem to find anything amiss. These little contretemps matter
not a whit to the great: they bite deep into the consciousness
of the young. I sometimes have that nightmare still.

The Governor's Comptroller had sent me, some days before, a
formidable list of the party's supply requirements. I said that
they must bring the luxuries with them, while we would provide
the essentials; and I assembled three hundred eggs before their
arrival, which I judged might last for a few days. After a
night at Kaptai they arrived in Rangamati and sat down to lunch
in the Circuit House. In the early afternoon I received a
message asking for more eggs. I went round to the Comptroller--
(who was also the Military Secretary).

"You had three hundred eggs this morning: what has happened
to them?"

"I suppose they have eaten them. We had a soufflé for
lunch. Our menus are prepared in Calcutta for weeks ahead, and
three hundred eggs don't go far, you know, not in a Government
House soufflé."

It was then that the Chittagong Hill Tracts Armed Police
had to go into action. I sent them into the villages with
orders to produce one thousand eggs by nightfall, which they
did. I did not conceal from His Excellency the act of
extortion (although the eggs were supposed to be paid for) which
his rapacious staff had made necessary, and H.E. replied, with a
very straight face, "Very well, we must ration ourselves for
eggs from now on."

After these involuntary defaults the tour went well. The
sun shone, no Chittagonian terrorist threw a bomb, the Governor
spotted several new birds and identified a rare tree unknown to
the Forest Officer. Sir John had said that he wanted to see
'the interior' of the district, so we took him and his entourage

out on an excursion as far from the headquarters as we could in the time available. We built four separate camps of bamboo huts, complete with banqueting halls and decorated archways. The party moved between them in a triumphal progress, on elephant-back and on foot; there is a ciné-film of it taken by one of the A.D.C.'s, preserved in the national film archives. I believe that it records the ceremonial salaam of upraised trunks with which the elephants greeted His Excellency every morning, and also the anti-climax of the procession. The last elephant in the line of twelve was an emergency reserve, and had the menial task of carrying from camp to camp, exposed to public view, two of those useful pieces of domestic furniture known as thunder-boxes. They were reserved for the use of the Governor and his sister: the rest of us had to make do with holes in the ground.

Earlier that year we had celebrated the Silver Jubilee of King George V. Rangamati was en fête: there were sports and tugs-of-war and boat races, and in the evening the houses and paths were lit with fairy lights, little wicks floating in oil-filled saucers. We planted flowering trees, a red tulip tree, a white bauhinia and a jacaranda, conspiring with nature to provide a patriotic display in the fullness of time. No doubt their flowers have now adjusted themselves to the national colours of Bangladesh.

In that year, too, our elder son David had been born in Shillong. My wife had to take him back to England, for the Hill Tracts were not ideal surroundings in which to raise an infant, and her gallant touring was at an end. There were parts of the district farther afield which I had not visited, and where it would have hard for her to follow.

The upper reaches of the Sangu and Matamuri are full of rapids, between creeper-hung cliffs. My boatmen, wearing orchids behind their ears in honour of the occasion, would shoot the rapids skilfully, poling the dug-out canoes over rocks, and roaring with laughter when I was soaked with spray. They would rest from time to time and pull out long leaves of tobacco, tear them down the mid-rib and roll them on their thighs into the longest, untidiest, sweetest-smelling cheroots I have ever experienced.

In the evening we would find a convenient sandbank, and my Mogh orderlies Mracha and Nilao, an inseparable and faithful pair, would jump out to cut bamboos with their <u>daos</u>. In ten minutes they had built a rough shelter, and gone to look for turtle eggs for supper. Then the villagers would begin to gather, and would sit round my fire in a silent shy ring, until the <u>zu</u> had circulated once or twice - it was opaque rice beer, which tasted like rough cider. This was followed by bottles of

Boat race at Rangamati, 1935

Elizabeth in dug-out canoe, 1935

David, 7 months, in Rangamati, 1936

the Deputy Commissioner's rum, and tongues would loosen and we would hear tales of how the world began, who made the rivers and the hills, the mysteries of life and death.

In these remote parts, several days march from the nearest hospital or dispensary, the villagers expected the Government, personified by me for the time being, to be a doctor too, or rather a witch doctor, a medicine man. My unqualified practice would certainly not have had the approval of the Government, if I had sought it; but I could not avoid it, for wherever I camped the villagers brought their sick to me to cure. It was faith healing, supported by magic. I used to take with me supplies of aspirin, fruit salts, and permanganate crystals, as well as anti-septic ointments, quinine and cough lozenges. Most of these had magic properties of a kind, and most of the symptoms brought to me were headaches, stomach aches or open sores. The aspirin relieved headaches and other pains, the fruit salts frothed and bubbled impressively and the water with which I bathed the sores was miraculously incarnadined by permanganate. I would make my patients swallow quinine, which was so bitter that it must be potent, and a cough lozenge was given as a bonus to take the taste away. In most cases, after my first aid, I urged - but without much confidence that the advice would be heeded - that the patient should go, or be carried to the nearest Government dispensary, where they would find a sub-assistant surgeon to follow up my quackery with more orthodox treatment. Their faith was as strong and touching as their manners were perfect. When I visited the villages again I was told of the wonderful cures I had achieved, never of the failures. In between my visits their panacea, I knew, was an opium pill.

Earlier D.C.'s had also enlisted magic to bolster their authority. The most legendary of these was Tom Lewin, known to the Moghs as Tongloyn and to the Lushais as Tangliena. He was an accomplished conjurer, and his most impressive trick was to allow himself to be shot, at ten paces, by a single-barrelled muzzle-loading gun, to demonstrate the invulnerability with which Queen Victoria had invested him. He would invite his audience to load the gun with a lead ball, which, on pretence of examining the weapon to see if they had done the job properly, he would somehow extract and replace with a wax ball. The gun was discharged, Tongloyn staggered back realistically, recovered himself and produced from his chest the lead ball which he had palmed. This demonstration was worth paying two years jhum tax to see, and guaranteed at least one year's good behaviour.

Under Tom Lewin's memorial at Demagiri, on the Lushai Hills frontier, I revived the practice of Border Meets with my opposite number in Assam. There we tried jointly cases of

Lushai customary law in which parties from both our districts were involved. The Lushais are agreeable people, tall, proud and courteous. In Assam some of them had come under the influence of Christian missionaries, who had caused them to dress in khaki shorts and imitation topees of woven straw, the badges of civilisation. I wish more could have taken refuge in my district, but there was only one ridge containing Lushai villages, where the men wore nothing but a short kilt, and their headmen were distinguised by magnificent home-woven plaids and drongo feathers on their unchristened heads.

It was in one of their villages on the Sajek ridge that I found a man sitting in the stocks, his feet through two holes in a large tree trunk sawn lengthwise in half. He was a lunatic, they said, but harmless, and had been kept in that restraint for some years. I ordered him to be released at once. He was bewildered by this sudden change, and sat down again as near as he could to his prison. I have no doubt that as soon as I left the village he went back willingly into the stocks. I was bound to release him, but was I right to do so? Kept near his home and under the eye of his family he was less of a danger to himself and to others; and he was happier and apparently better fed than he would have been in an asylum or hospital in strange surroundings. The choice between justice and expediency is often difficult.

I used to take a portable gramophone with me on tour, with a mixture of music hall and classical records. The Lushais especially enjoyed an impromptu concert. Instrumental music did not impress them much. They and other hill tribes made their own queer sounds out of the bamboo pipes, which inspired them to shuffling dances; but they listened entranced to the human voice coming out of a box. They particularly liked a simple song by Jack Hulbert, "The flies crawled up the window", in the middle of which he would break into an infectious laugh, whereat the whole village rocked with merriment, and demanded it again and again. How pleased Jack Hulbert would have been to see the pleasure he gave in that far corner of the hills.

However far one went, the post never failed to catch up. It was inspiring to see His Majesty's Mail threading its way at a jog trot through the wildest country, over the shoulder of a dak-runner armed only with spear, to which a couple of bells were attached to warn off unfriendly animals.

Urgent official letters would be brought to me on tour by a swift-footed policeman. It tried one's patience to open a cover marked "Immediate", delivered by a panting orderly who had followed my ten days' march into the jungle, and find that it was from some babu in Calcutta calling for the prompt submission of a statement of licensed cinemas in my district, or an immediate explanation why no new motor vehicle registrations had been reported for five years. There was not a cinema or a motor car within a hundred miles.

The headmen had to supply me with porters who were paid at a fixed rate, to which I added a packet of cigarettes for each man as a bonus. They also had to provide me with free accommodation wherever I halted for the night, for tents were an impediment on a long, continually-moving tour, and inspection, bungalows were rare. Often the lodging would be a freshly built sweet-smelling bamboo <u>basha</u>, stocked with sections of thick bamboo containing water for my bath, a performance which all the village children would observe with curiosity, peering through the slats of the hut. Sometimes it was an old, abandoned jhum, house which I shared with rats that ran across my feet all night or a cockroach-infested sampan tied to the river bank.

There were also certain social conventions, on the proper observance of which, sometimes, the honour of the Raj might seem to depend. A headman would send a party of his friends to meet me a mile or so out of the village with bottles of <u>zu</u>, varying in potency but refreshing as the morning grew hot after a twelve mile march. On reaching the headman's house there would be more <u>zu</u>, a pitcher full of it in the middle of his ceremonial platform, with a straw sticking out of its neck. One was invited to partake, while the headman and reception committee looked on: one could not in courtesy decline. The rule, with local variations, was that the pitcher had to be drained by the guest of honour crouching over it and sucking upwards, but without removing his mouth from the straw. If I failed in this, much of my authority would have evaporated.

There seemed to be nearly a gallon of the stuff. As I rose breathless from the completed task, there was the headman's lovely daughter kneeling before me with a bamboo cup full of rice spirit. The "moonshine" of the Hill Tracts is warming in an emergency, but should not be rolled round the tongue: it tastes like petrol with a dash of castor oil.

"Drink this, please," said the headman's daughter, like a hospital nurse. I would take a sip. Ugh. "No, you drink some" "No, you drink all". Between us we would manage to spill most of it while the assembled elders shook with diplomatic mirth.

"Now, your honour," the headman would say, "shall we dicuss that matter of the jhum tax?"

"Not on your life, maung gri; not until I have slept this off."

Elephants formed a large part of our lives. Trained elephants are companionable and full of character, and, apart from their size, would make good domestic pets. We certainly became attached to our two police elephants. When Lal Bahadur was baggage carrier, the mahout would unload him at the end of the day's march and throw him his shackle chain. He would pick this up and sling it in the crook of his trunk; he would then look round for me, and when found would follow me like a dog round the village until I gave him his reward of a juicy papaya or a bunch of bananas. Then he would find the nearest stream and lie down in it on his side until the mahout came to give him his bath. "Turn over!" the mahout would say, and Lal Bahadur would roll over onto the other side, while the mahout scrubbed him like a baby.

But this was Lal Bahadur off duty: he was a professional government servant, too, and especially so in a kheddah. Reports had come in of serious damage to crops by wild elephants on the edge of a forest reserve. It was really the business of the Forest Department to keep under control the fauna to which they gave sanctuary, but for some reason they were unwilling that year to arrange a kheddah - the capture of elephants in a stockade - so I decided to do it myself. I read up all the manuals and literature on the subject, and engaged a kheddah contractor from Chittagong. On this first occasion I paid the price of inexperience. The contractor had other more profitable work on hand, and postponed my kheddah until too late in the season. Very few elephants were caught, but the contractor pocketed his fee.

By the following year I was wiser. The contractor tried to economise by building a stockade with thin walls, and hoped to discourage the elephants from charging it by means of vicious spikes pointing inwards. This was not in the Queensberry Rules: I made him remove the spikes, build a double wall and make small openings through which we might rescue any very young elephants caught in the drive, before they were trampled by the herd in the stockade.

The operation itself was skilful and exciting. For days a large herd had been manoeuvred gently towards the wings of the stockade, which were of lighter construction, stretching far into the forest. At the same time the tuskers of the herd, which are troublesome and dangerous in a kheddah, were being gradually separated from the females and tuskless males.

On the appointed night I was sitting on a platform above the stockade. The silence was eerie, broken only by the distant 'sawing' of a leopard. Suddenly, about a mile away in the forest, all hell broke loose. With yells, gongs, crackers and flaring torches the herd was stampeded, driven between the long wings into the stockade, and the trap was dropped.

The pandemonium and the wild trumpeting within was fearsome. The terrified animals tried to charge the walls of the stockade, but could not get their shoulders to it, as a trench had been dug round inside. We managed to rescue two small elephants through the openings. Next morning the herd was quiet but restless. Water and fodder were passed through the openings, but were not touched.

Then Lal Bahadur's turn came. The trap was raised and, with his brave mahout astride his neck - toes behind each great ear to steer him - Lal Bahadur entered the stockade, and trumpeted a challenge.

'Now, my darling, my pearl, steady, go carefully' said the mahout, in elephant language.

One stout-hearted old lady accepted the challenge and came forward. The rest made way, as if to allow room for single combat. There was a short, fierce tussle, with trunks inter-twined, but Lal Bahadur's tusks were too much for her. She turned, and he chased her round the stockade, belabouring her with his trunk. A few days later the captured elephants, who had meanwhile accepted food and water, were brought out, one by one, and tethered each beside a trained elephant. The process of indoctrination had begun.

We caught thirty-six saleable elephants, a profitable catch, for Government and for the contractor. I had the pick the bunch for the police, and chose an eighteen-year-old youngster, to replace the pensioned Daisy. Within a fortnight the new recruit had learned to obey simple commands.

Before I left the Hill Tracts, I was sent to Chittagong for a few months, to have charge of that district while its Collector was on leave. I realised then that I had been too long away from civilisation. Sometimes for weeks on end I had little chance of speaking my own language, except to myself.

I had already acquired, on previous short visits to Chittagong, a reputation of the wild man from the hills. When I entered the Club bar my first evening there, I imagined that people were looking curiously and rather anxiously at me. I felt like Caliban. How polished these men and women are, I thought. How easily and brilliantly they talk; I can never hope to join in their conversation. I had better keep quiet.

Two whiskies soon corrected that inferiority, and then it would have been hard to stop me talking - or even singing. Before long I was leading the choruses in that talented company. A man at the piano (I remember) played 'chopsticks' standing on his head; a military policeman, ex-Foreign Legionnaire, sang French barrack-room songs alone in a corner, because he felt the 'cafard' coming on; I tore down curtains, waved them like a banner, and gave a rendering of the Red Flag.

There was an emergency in Chittagong at that time, and a battalion of Gurkhas was stationed there, of which the adjutant entered the bar when all this was going on. His first impression was that revolution had started, and he retired hastily to warn his junior officers against fraternisation with the new civil power.

Next morning I remembered that I was now the Collector of an important district, not Maung Pooh Bah in the jungle. For the rest of my time in Chittagong I hope I conducted myself with decorum and did my duty.

Soon afterwards I was due for home leave - and it was high time too.

5

'Dilli dur ast'

I left Bengal in 1937. During the next twenty-one years I often
went back there, but our adopted home, the place of my family's
childhood, as it had been of my own, was henceforth in upper
India. It was salutary and refreshing for us to have a change
of scene, among a different people, speaking a different
language, and to experience the dramatic contrasts of a
different climate.

In upper India February is the perfect month. It is
neither winter, nor summer, nor spring: it is its own season, a
glimpse of paradise vouchsafed to man and beast, to sustain them
during the purgatory of the months ahead. Spring comes and goes
hardly noticed. One morning the <u>neem</u> trees have put out their
green leaves before the yellow have fallen, and for a few days
the air is heavy with the scent of mango blossom. Then begins
to fall the monotonous hammer of the copper-smith bird: the
crescendo of the <u>koel</u> rises to a scream; all living things move
more slowly and seek the shade. Men and women committed to the
plains recite the 121st Psalm, or some equivalent prayer, and
brace themselves for a long siege. A hot wind rides in from the
desert like an invading army, its impact a physical assault.
For weeks and months the sky is hidden behind a lurid pall of
dust, and night brings little or no relief from the obsessive
heat. In June small clouds begin to gather above the South
Western horizon, to swell and approach, but vanish again like
mirages, sickening with hope deferred. At last, with storms of
spectacular violence, the monsoon deluge bursts, and all nature
is washed and green and breathes again. For a few days cool air
and the smell of damp earth are blessings beyond price, until
saturation and humidity bring new miseries – prickly heat and
plagues of winged and stinging insects – harder to bear than
those of the furnace days: or, on a more dramatic scale, if the
elements have been immoderate, floods, famine and sickness
stalk the land.

But, one day in October, the annual miracle recurs, for
which all endurance had been worth while. A shiver, a sudden
freshness tells that the air current has moved round into the
north, and now flows down from the Himalayan snows, a promise of

at least five months of the finest climate in the world.

After I had been in the Chittagong Hill Tracts for nearly three years - and for much of that time living alone - I was beginning to resemble some jungle creature hanging by its tail from a tree. I therefore had a problem; and so, no doubt, had the Government of Bengal with whom I had by now served for nine years. It was probably in the best interest of both Government and of its servant when I was summoned to New Delhi, for a two-year appointment as under-secretary in the newly formed Communications Department of the Government of India. Delhi, in fact, was to be our home for the next fifteen years.

'Dilli dur ast' - Delhi is far away, the vicereoys of the Mogul emperors used to say, in their best Persian, when they were inclined to ignore some command from the Peacock Throne.

It was far away from Rangamati, in those 'blue remembered hills' beyond the Bay of Bengal. It was nearly a thousand miles from Calcutta. It was a new and exciting adventure for me as I stepped out into the frosty December night from Delhi railway station, near the Kashmir Gate - still showing the scars of John Nicholson's assault - and drove past the flaring lights and clamour of the Chandni Chowk, under the walls of Akbar's Red Fort to the eighth imperial city beside the Jumna, the modern architectural wonder of New Delhi.

In a sense it was like coming home. As a boy in 1911 I had lived in tents by the Jumna bank during the Coronation Durbar, and I had seen the foundation stone of the new capital of India laid by the King-Emperor, Pancham (the fifth) George, whose long reign had only just ended. That stone was later quietly removed from the swampy site originally chosen, to higher ground near the Ridge.

From there Sir Edwin Lutyens and Sir Herbert Baker had mounted their elephants and surveyed the ancient landmarks, peering over the top of low babul-thorn scrub to plan their avenues and vistas. This would lead the eye to the Jama Masjid; that would be directed on Humayun's Tomb; and would it be possible to let the Viceroy have a view of the Purana Qila, or the more distant Kutb Minar?

Lutyens was to design the superbly proportioned Viceroy's House, with its Mogul garden. Baker planned the magnificent rose-red twin Secretariat buildings, with their far-from-functional pillared porticos and cornices, on top of the wide sweep of the Ramp. On those cornices and that ramp, Lutyens and Baker fell out, like Gilbert and Sullivan over the pattern of a carpet; for they masked and diminished the full effect of Lutyens' masterpiece.

Clustered round the foot of this acropolis were the houses of the officials - 'Baker's ovens', some of them were called -

each in a miniature park, lining a labyrinth of roads which
fanned out in all directions, and all so alike that a newcomer
could lose his way hopelessly in them at night.

The grand design had barely been completed when we first
saw it. Work was still going on, having been commanded by Lady
Willingdon a few years before, to convert the wilderness which
had surrounded the tombs of the Lodi Kings into a beautiful
informal garden, including an open-air theatre - a favourite
playground for children and their attendants.

For Elizabeth, left behind in Calcutta, it had been a case
of 'pay, pack and follow'; but by the time that she had joined
me, a month later, a private house had been found, beside the
Lodi Gardens. It was brand new, built to the design of its
Indian owner, and its marble floors were inlaid with splendid
arabesques. We were not used to the winter cold of northern
India, and had to cover the marble with a carpet, which our
disappointed landlord considered a reflection on his taste.

I owed my transfer to Delhi to a senior Bengali colleague,
Satyanendra Nath Roy, with whom I had earlier worked in
Calcutta, and who was now Secretary of the new Department of
Communications of the Government of India. After this act of
provincial nepotism, S.N. Roy and his wife befriended us in many
ways, finding us our house and showing us the ropes in the new
environment. There were several S.N. Roys in the talented
Brahmo Samaj community of Bengal; this one was known,
demi-officially, as S.N. Roy Number One, until he was more
adequately distinguished by a knighthood later on, but to his
many friends he was affectionately known simply as 'Buru', Elder
Brother. He was one of the most equable, patient, clear-headed,
hard-working civil servants I have ever met, and he set me a
much-needed example in the high standard of his own work, for
which I have never ceased to be grateful.

The Communications Department had come about as a
reorganistion of two other departments. It was the engine which
drove, or rather gave motive power, to several important wheels,
called misleadingly 'attached offices'. The difficulty was to
keep them attached, and to prevent them from flying off in
directions of their own choice. The Department was their
governess - it served and guided them, but, without letting it
become too apparent, it controlled them too. It fought their
continual battles with the Finance Department for ways and
means, represented them as champion and apologist in the
Legislative Assembly, and provided a conveyor-belt of proposal,
argument, decision and action, between them and the
Governor-General's Executive Council.

The attached offices included the well-established and
powerful Railway Board, and younger, vigorous, expanding bodies

like the Civil Aviation Directorate and All-India Radio. They were presided over by some impressive and colourful characters. Frederick Tymms was Director of Civil Aviation. He had gained his wings with the Royal Flying Corps, and was to become in due course a world authority on the organisation of air routes and the international law of the air. At that time he was engaged in establishing a network of aerodromes in India. His quiet manner was deceptive. He had the appearance and, in negotiation, the tenacity of a terrier.

Very different was Lionel Fielden, the first Controller of Broadcasting in India. He had a flowing mane of hair and an aggressively artistic temperament. He seemed to have a persecution mania, being convinced that, with few exceptions, everyone with whom he had official relations was conspiring to frustrate him. One of the exceptions was Sir Percy Grigg, the Finance Member of the Governor General's Council, himself an importation from England who did not try to hide his disgruntlement with all things Indian, and was not an easy man to work with. Lionel Fielden - not averse to a little conspiracy on his own account - with Grigg's sympathy and support, no doubt hoped to outflank his imaginary opponents. Despite these handicaps Fielden was a stimulating character, whether in alliance or in opposition, who succeeded in giving a fine start to All-India Radio. He was greatly helped, on the technical side, by Cecil Goyder, his brilliant Chief Engineer, whose services the B.B.C. had also loaned to the Government of India.

A particular object of Fielden's odium and suspicions was my own immediate superior, Astad Dinshaw Gorwala, the Deputy Secretary, a Parsee of great ability and originality of mind. Gorwala has since made his mark in many fields; and especially, after he retired from the I.C.S., as a fearless critic of the independent Government of India, dipping a pseudonymous pen in an acid worthy of the letters of Junius.

There was a great deal of talent around in the higher echelons of the civil service, and also some fine examples of that civil service phenomenon, the clever Secretary who never grows up. Our own Member of Council was just such an overgrown under-secretary, although he must have had other virtues which had hoisted him to ministerial rank. He had an analytical mind, but a too meticulous itch to amend. He could not accept the simplest draft without fiddling with the construction and punctuation, until the original meaning and argument were hopelessly obscured. The style of the letter, one felt, were more important to him than the achievement of its object.

More pragmatic but possessed of the same kind of self-sufficiency was Girja Shankar Bajpai, Secretary of another

Department, who forthrightly declared 'Give me three good stenographers, and I have no need of deputy or under-secretaries!' It was not until I came to realise that it was under-secretaries who kept the wheels of government running that I understood how necessary it was for our experienced seniors to instil this sense of inferiority among the lower orders. Bajpai redeemed himself in my eyes by what seemed to me an engaging eccentricity - or perhaps it was simply good horticulture. He had a garden containing one thousand rose bushes, specially ordered from Europe. On the principle that in India the best years of a rose's life are its first four, he uprooted two hundred and fifty of them every year and replaced them with further imports. We could have done with some of Bajpai's rejects in our own garden.

I was no longer a jungle-cock crowing in the Hill Tracts: I had become a slave of the File; and I slaved, for the first few months, in an ice box, the only room in the North Block of the Imperial Secretariat which had neither window nor artificial heat. In the dry cold of northern India which penetrates to the bone, I sat clad in a jersey, an overcoat and two pairs of socks, stamping to keep myself warm. A few months later I would be gasping in an airless oven. There was a primitive air-conditioning system, through the ducts of which a faint odour of garlic sometimes stirred. A cynical colleague explained: 'Didn't you know? When it breaks down they make three chaprassies lie at one end and blow through it until it is mended.'

The Secretariat File was no longer the portentous compilation which Lord Curzon had described, gathering weight and volume as it progressed through the corridors of government, in ponderous, elephantine majesty. It had become almost streamlined. A clerk assembled and flagged all the documents, correspondence and connected files; an assistant - one grade up in the office staff - summarised the contents; the under-secretary made his recommendation and, if necessary, drafted a letter for approval.

Red-lettered was the day, and proud was the under-secretary when his signature was subscribed, without further material comment, by three others, of the Deputy Secretary, the Secretary and the Member of Council, and occasionally, with a single initial, by the Viceroy himself. The humble submission had gone right up the stairway to the summit, and Olympian Zeus had nodded.

I was fortunate in my senior assistant, Venkatachellum, a south Indian Hindu. Although at the time he was in a clerical post, he had sat, a few years before, for the I.C.S. examination in India, and had been unsuccessful by one place only. If it had been an open examination he would have made the grade, but in those days special reservation had to be made for Muslim candidates. I was delighted to find, some years later, after Independence, that merit had its reward, and that the assistant who had first guided me along the paths of secretariat procedure, had risen to become a full secretary to the Government of India in a new Ministry.

It was not all paper work in a Secretariat post; we sometimes got away from our desks for special duties. On one memorable occasion - when there must have been a temporary shortage of more senior officers in the Department - I flew with Tymms and others of the Civil Aviation Directorate to Karachi, to represent the Central Government at the opening of the great new aerial gateway of India, the Drigh Road Airport. There were still sad reminders visible there in 1938 of the ill-fated airship, R 101, its mooring mast and the gigantic hangar which it never occupied.

In April the Government moved to Simla. The process took ten days, for this was no skeleton staff affair. Senior officers took ten days leave, and under-secretaries were left to rule the land, and to supervise the removal and elevation of all the files and impedimenta of government to the cool, exhilarating, bustling city 7000 feet up in the foothills of the Himalayas. That year was the last of an era. Simla was still gay, but few had any doubt that, this year or next, we might be at war. It was the gaiety of the Duchess of Richmond's ball before Waterloo.

We under-secretaries were responsible for co-ordinating the War Books of our various departments - massive tomes, about twelve square feet in surface area when open, and increasing in volume every day. I suppose our ideas of security were rather primitive, for my copy followed me, wrapped in a red cloth, on the head of a coolie as I clip-clopped on horseback along the mall to my office, and back again in the evening. Sometimes the cloth would come adrift and then the War Book, with its menacing implications, would be exposed to the public gaze.

Meanwhile the dance went on. Elizabeth and I and our young David occupied a flat in a government tenement, Craig Dhu, which had a fine view of the river Sutlej in the plains below. The ridge on which Simla was built is a true watershed, dividing the river systems of the Indus and Ganges valleys. It was said that if, standing on that ridge, you happened to spit in one direction it would be an increment to the Bay of Bengal; in the other, it would benefit the Arabian Sea. Whether or not this had anything to do with the choice of Simla for India's summer capital, it was certianly ideally situated for remote control, remoter even than Delhi, hidden in the scorching dust haze of the plains, out of sight and temporarily out of mind.

For family transport we depended on rickshaws. These two-seater man-drawn carriages were hired, when required by ordinary mortals, from public rickshaw stands; but the private rickshaws of the great were pulled by liveried teams of four - sometimes five jhampanies, who shouted arrogantly 'bacchyo!' - 'Look out for yourselves!' - as they cantered downhill, or panted and groaned to excite the compassion of the more heavy-weight passengers, as they toiled up the slope in the opposite direction. At night, as the rickshaws wound their way up the hill paths with guests to dinner parties or dances, at Viceregal Lodge, maybe, or Snowdon, the Commander-in-Chief's house, their lamps illumimated the hillsides like strings of glow-worms.

Simla had always been a kind of holiday workshop. In 1938, while the rest of the world was on the brink of a precipice, the holiday mood seemed more than usually artificial; not consciously escapist, but because on this Himalayan ridge, nothing that anyone, not even the King-Emperor's representative, could do was likely to affect the issue, there was an intense concentration on carrying on with business, but recreation was also ample. I did not count the number of tennis courts to the acre, but there were a great many - and few flat acres - and some of the courts were built out on impossible projections over the perpendicular khud side. The tennis was energetic: the rarified air, which helped the secretariat to think more clearly and coolly, also caused the balls to bounce higher, and the players were breathless until they became acclimatised, but were refreshed at sundown by drinks cooled in Himalayan snow. Then, on to the Gaiety Theatre or to its satellite club, the Green Room - the bijou theatre to which, at the age of six, I had been taken by my mother, impressive in a frou-frou of Edwardian satin, to see my first play, 'H.M.S. Pinafore'; or to splendid white tie dances at the covered Canadian Tennis courts of the United Service Club, where the bachelor society of Simla used to entertain. The Black Hearts, our hosts, wore cloaks lined with crimson silk; or, if any member had fallen from grace, and was living in open matrimony, their cloaks were lined with penitential white. Champagne flowed, and there were crackers and paper caps imported from Paris.

Or we would ride out at week-ends, round Jakko with its monkey temple. Simla was frequented by two kinds of monkeys during the summer months, just as it was the headquarters of two governments. There were the common brown hanumans who - coincidentally, of course, - arrived each year at about the same time that the Government of the Punjab came up from Lahore; and the proud and beautiful silver-grey and black langurs who appeared about a week later, with the Government of India.

Beyond the hills of Jakko and Shali was the Hindustan-Tibet road, and Mashobra where, at 8000 feet or so the Viceroy had another mountain retreat. From here the paths beckoned along a choice of ridges, leafy or barren, up and down, always nearer to the snows; to Narkunda, to Naldera or to Carignano where, on the Simla Golf course you must drive your ball straight if you were not to lose it in a valley three thousand feet below.

On the way to Mashobra was Dukani, the house of Sir Edward Buck, the historian of Simla. It was an honour to be invited to one of his 'sniffnics'. His guests were paired off to wander over miles of hillside following lines of string from which were suspended little bags, full of curious smells to be identified. The game ended at sunset when at any rate the more earnest competitors had straggled back with the answers; but there were no prizes, except good company and the mountain air. Apart from a few foreign diplomats and some holiday-makers the Simla community consisted almost entirely of officials British and Indian, and of those who ministered to their needs. It was a happy and friendly community on the whole, especially - and perhaps surprisingly - in the close quarters of our own multi-storeyed lodging house Craig Dhu. There we met Joe Lentaigne, who was later to command the Chindits in Burma, after General Wingate's death; Lentaigne was an active soldier by temperament, but at that time he was eating out his heart as a chair-borne major in the Defence Department. There we met many of our life-long friends and, closest of all, the Bayleys whose family matched and grew up with ours. Vernon was a police officer with a distinguished record of service in the Punjab and in Delhi, and Viola, a lovely person whose acting then entranced Simla, and whose books have since delighted generations of teenagers.

In October the great migration was put into reverse, and we descended to the plains. We were working against time now. India was not prepared for war and, although the news of Munich had come to us in Simla, most of us realised that the only thankfulness we should feel was for a short respite in which to prepare for the inevitable.

I was lowest on the list of under-secretaries entitled to an official house in New Delhi that year, and fortunate that I had no choice, but had to take the oldest. It was therefore not a 'Baker's oven' but a bungalow designed for their own all-the-year-round habitation by the Public Works engineers who had built New Delhi, Number Five, York Road was to be our home for nine years, until Independence and after. It was spacious and cool, with high ceilings, thick walls, wide verandahs and a large garden full of flowers for most of the year; jonquils at

The bungalow at 5 York Road, New Delhi, 1937

Christmas, with poinsettias; peach blossom and roses in February, and a wealth of English annuals in between; then bright, starry portulaca in the summer, zinnias and balsam and flowering shrubs in the monsoon. There were shady trees for the children to climb and swing from, and a grove of tall blue gums at the end of the drive, on the branches of which bees would swarm. Gypsies came to remove the black wedges of comb which hung from the branches, leaving us a few pounds of pungent wild honey as tribute. Peacocks would do their courting on our lawn or roof and, I do not regret to say, provided us more than once with our Christmas dinner. Their cacophonous love calls were a horrid contrast with the gentle carrooing of Elizabeth's white fantail pigeons.

David grew up in Number Five, and our three other children were all born within a mile of it; so that the earliest memories of all but the youngest must be of that pleasant paradise.

Our shopping centre was in the concentric rings of modern Connaught Circus, but we were surrounded by ancient history. We explored the countryside and the ruins of the Seven Cities, the Jumna as far as Okhla and the canal banks beyond; the Ridge and other relics of the Mutiny in Old Delhi; Tughlakabad, and the mysterious semi-circle of massive stone steps at Suraj Kund. We rode across the open plain towards Palam, covered then with the crumbling monuments of ancient empires – and now by a cosmopolitan rash of chanceries and other diplomatic buildings. We hunted jackal round the overgrown, abandoned amphitheatre where George V. and his Queen-Empress had sat in state.

The Delhi Gymkhana Club was too new an institution at that time to have acquired the aura and patina necessary to attract a regular club membership, so that we and our friends used to gather socially in each others' houses, and on Sunday mornings there was often to be found on our lawn a subversion of under-secretaries (if that is the right collective noun) and their wives, drinking beer and scandalously dissecting their seniors. It is interesting now to recall that among them was a future Cabinet Minister of Pakistan and a future Indian ambassador.

When we made our way up the hill again in April, the atmosphere in Simla was more serious and subdued. The drama of that year, as it unfolded daily, and what lay hidden in the future, were endlessly discussed. We knew that the postponement of war had been bought at a heavy price. Some, but not many, hoped that the menace of Hitler would prove to be a gigantic bluff, but that hope was fading fast. The political parties in India were waiting and watching, and so were the Princes, the rulers of the Indian States.

There was little doubt about the Princes' loyalty if the crisis should come, but a crucial point had been reached in the constitutional discussions about their future. A new federal constitution was on the anvil which would have enabled a united India to advance to self-government and dominion status. The Princes' States accounted for a substantial part of the area and population of the sub-continent, and would have provided a balancing factor between the main political parties, whose composition reflected the irreconcilable religious divisions of the people. With infinite patience the Viceroy, Lord Linlithgow, had been explaining, negotiating, persuading. Some Princes had already provisionally acceded; others remained to be convinced. As the likelihood of a world war increased, so did the certainty that, if it came, all constitutional proposals would be put in abeyance, and whatever emerged at the end of it would not be the same. So even the Princes who had accepted federation on the terms proposed, conditionally or otherwise, now asked to be relieved of any commitment. The unity of India was one of the first casualties of the war.

For those who tried to carry on with their daily work, remote and ineffectual, at a time of momentous decisions which would affect all our lives, it was a period of frustration and restlessness. When war was declared there was something like a sense of relief. But Delhi – and Simla – were, in truth far away from it all.

Meanwhile my family's allotted home was one of a cluster of small houses called The Park, clinging to a hillside of Chhota Simla. To reach it we crossed the Combermere Bridge, where Kipling's philanderer first saw the phantom rickshaw, and we passed Peliti's restaurant into which he had dashed for a glass of cherry brandy, to steady his nerves. The terraced banks which surrounded our new quarters were covered with wild dahlias and slippery with pine needles. Among our neighbours were Bijoo Nehru, a nephew of Jawaharlal's, and his Hungarian wife, Forey. Another beautiful Hungarian lived next door, married to a Bengali whose job was Inspector of Lighthouses – a nice example (one thousand miles from the sea) of bureaucratic remote control.

Here four-year-old David discovered the delights of playing with the telephone in idle moments, and one day managed to connect himself with the private line of the Commander-in-Chief. Fortunately he did not succeed in speaking directly to the great man himself, for in that case 'Snowdon' might have erupted in flames: but a puzzled ADC, trying to identify the mysterious caller, heard Elizabeth's brisk summons: 'Come along now, David. That's quite enough telephoning for today.' We were not easily allowed to forget the incident.

Just before the outbreak of war I had joined the Viceroy's staff as Deputy Private Secretary. I was happily unaware at the time of the tug-o-war in which I had been the rope. Bengal had originally parted with my services without demur, but had the right to recall me after two years which by now were nearly completed. On the other hand, the Viceroy needed to enlarge his Private Secretary's Office, and weight will tell. A rival candidate, I heard later, was Penderel Moon, a brilliant and stimulating character, and a Fellow of All Souls, who eventually outlasted nearly all of his British I.C.S. colleagues in the service of the Government of India. The Vicereine disapproved of married junior officers on the staff. Of the alternatives, therefore, one was a bachelor, but argumentative: the other was more conventional but married. If, as is possible, the matter was decided by the spin of a coin, there then began for me a period of such intense interest and rewarding labour that I am still astounded at my luck that the coin fell right for me.

History will give Lord Linlithgow his due, for he was one of the great Viceroys. It must have been a cruel disappointment to him that all his patient work to make possible the federal constitution which would have kept independent India united, and which came so near to success, was swept away at the outbreak of war. Without his courage, foresight and firmness over the next four years India could never have played the part she did in the struggle that was to come, on her own frontiers and overseas. He was the first of the splended trio of Viceroys who built the last uphill miles of the road to India's independence, and he laid the foundation of it.

He was regarded by many who did not know him well as an aloof and unsympathetic character, than which nothing could have been further from the truth. He may have lacked what public relations men call 'charisma', but possessed a peculiarly Scottish sincerity and frankness which made him sometimes seem abrupt. He was immensely tall and had a physical handicap which made it difficult for him to turn his head, and this may have given rise to the fallacy of his aloofness in public: it also caused him, when speaking to those beside him, to turn his body towards them, so that they knew his whole attention was theirs.

He was devoted to his family, his wife and three daughters, and twin sons at the war, one of whom was to be a prisoner for most of it. He treated his staff like his family, and when I was accepted into the family circle, I found him human, friendly and entertaining, with an often boisterous sense of fun.

In the early months of the war there was a fairly rapid turnover of the viceregal staff. Regimental duties took away Military Secretaries and ADCs. Among them was George Burns, a cheerful and reassuring companion in all circumstances, whom

Linlithgow used aptly to describe as 'a hundred per cent eupeptic'. He won a Military Cross in what must have been almost the first real action of the war.

My own work was mainly with Gilbert Laithwaite, the Private Secretary. It is impossible to do justice to Gilbert in a few lines. I learned more from him in three-and-a-half years than from any man I know, and in all that time, of great pressure on him, there was never a hard word between us. Very rarely there was a flicker of reproof, well deserved but gone like summer lightning, although I must often have tried him sorely. His standards were of the highest, his memory prodigious and his output enormous. Only the champion stenographer of India, the faithful Iyer, a Madrassi with a horrible squint, could keep up with the speed of his dictation, in which he would seldom pause, putting in a parenthesis where others might ponder over a semi-colon. He disciplined his mind and body, but could relax splendidly, a convivial companion and the best of hosts: never without a carnation in his buttonhole, always dressed in the smartest and thickest of suits, whether in winter or Indian summer. He was the perfect Private Secretary in that he could enter into his master's mind and interpret his thoughts in the words he would have used.

The Assistant Private Secretary and I had our own duties, but we were often consulted and never excluded from the news of great events and secrets of state. In fact we often knew them before anyone else, for we alone worked the special cipher for messages between the Viceroy and the Secretary of State for India. When a signal from Whitehall began: 'Take strong whisky peg before continuing', we obediently broke off to do so, for some startling development was about to be revealed. On one such occasion it was to warn Linlithgow that Winston Churchill had decided to send Sir Stafford Cripps on his Mission to discuss the constitutional future with the Indian political leaders.

We read the ribald comments of our masters in the margin of letters from the almost equally great. 'The silly old buzzfuzz' was one which found its way (accidentally I am sure) into the printed records of Viceregal correspondence. We were privileged to meet important visitors, and at one time there was a continuous stream of Indian politicians and Princes to the Viceroy's House in New Delhi or to Viceregal Lodge in Simla.

Once, when Mahatma Gandhi called, Gilbert Laithwaite, who had damaged himself in a fall from his pony a day or two before, was supposed to be in bed. I was about to do duty for him, as the Mahatma arrived, when Gilbert was observed hurrying along the path from his house, his head swathed in bandages. 'Ah, Sir Gilbert,' said the Mahatma, 'what happened to you? Do I see

Lord Linlithgow and Sir Gilbert Laithwaite, Simla, 1941

from your appearance that you have been practising some violence' 'Mr Gandhi, you behold in me a convert to non-violence' replied Gilbert. 'It is no use!' said the Mahatma, grinning broadly, while his secretary, Mahadev Desai, picked from his shawl marigold petals shed by the garlands of the faithful, 'You have been converted perforce.'

One of the duties of the Private Secretary's Office was to draft the Viceroy's many speeches. Laithwaite undertook the important political speeches; his deputy and assistant dealt with the rest. I soon learned that the less time one had to prepare a draft, the better it usually was. Once a speech for a school prizegiving was sprung on us an hour before the event. This was a more serious affair than the unveiling of a statue or the presentation of regimental colours, for some of the boys might be so impressed by the occasion that they would remember what was said. I took lunchtime off to compose a draft. It had to be approved, typed on appropriate paper and the pages tied with blue silk ribbon. The result was inspiring, though short, and I was proud of it. So was the Viceroy, who said that it nearly moved him to tears as he delivered it. On another occasion, since the Viceroy was to address some learned High Court Judges, I was bold enough to insert a Latin quotation in the draft. 'You had better go and see that H.E. is happy about that Latin' said Gilbert.

'Oh yes, quite happy, John,' said H.E. 'Fine stuff, Virgil.' I dared not explain to him that the quotation was from Horace; and so, to the amazement of his scholarly audience, the alcaics were duly delivered, full of false quantities, as if they were rolling hexameters.

The Viceroy had a large parish, and he was often on tour. As work had to go on wherever he was, he took a cipher staff and part of the Private Secretary's office with him. His special train was a smart affair of five or six coaches, shining white and well equipped, though not air-conditioned. In summer, blocks of ice would be loaded at intervals into the compartments, and the fans playing on the ice made a grateful breeze. I had a bed-cum-office suite to myself, but I had to give up my bathroom, to be converted into a bar for the ADCs, who would otherwise have had to walk along the corridor of Their Excellencies' coach to the dining car for a drink. It had the advantage that I had not far to go for mine. We dined together, and the Mess of 'Viceroy's Camp' on rail shared a privilege with His Majesty's ships at sea, of being permitted for reasons of stability to drink the Royal Toast seated.

The train must have been a fine sight as it wound its way through the length and breadth of India, through the jungles and plateaux of the Deccan, over the Western Ghats, across great rivers and along the sea coast. At every hundred yards or so stood a village watchman or policeman facing outwards with spear or gun, and flaring torches held aloft at night. Every two or three hours we drew up at a station, and telegrams and urgent papers were handed in. The hours of work, therefore tended to be longer than at headquarters, for the day might begin at 3 a.m. and go on until after midnight.

For travelling in those parts of India which were served by a metre gauge line, the Viceroy had a special miniature train, which had been built for the royal visit to India in 1911. Except for elbow-room it was as well equipped and comfortable as the standard gauge trian, but when we drew up at a ceremonial platform to visit, say, the State of some Prince in Kathiawar, H.E. had to be careful not to knock his hat off as he stepped out of the train, and the ADCs not to disarrange the plumes on their helmets.

It was not all hard work, not at any rate during the first year of the war. The Viceroy occasionally took a few days holiday for shikar, for which his enthusiasm was boundless as he was a fine shot and fisherman. Indeed one could say that he seldom missed an opportunity of having a shot at something, and I believe he always carried a catapult in his pocket. A good part of the first day after Lord Linlithgow's arrival in Simla would be spent in chasing the monkeys out of the grounds of Viceregal Lodge. H.E. would adopt the attitude of a stalker on the moors, and close behind him, with a .22 rifle would crawl the ADC-on-duty. 'Keep that damn thing away from my backside' H.E. would say. 'It might do me a serious injury.'

I once took some papers to his study, and found him standing at the window, catapult in hand, looking down at the lawn below. The St. John's Ambulance Brigade were practising there, and the wife of one of his Members of Council was bending down with her back to him, bandaging a dummy stretcher case.

'It's a wonderful target, John,' he said, 'but I suppose there are some temptations one must resist.'

Once, in Kashmir, we had been taken to see the Mogul gardens in Shalimar, and the party was walking on either side of an artificial channel of water in which small fountains were playing at intervals. Ping-pong balls and an occasional egg were dancing on top of each jet of spray. H.E. could not resist that temptation. Out came the catapult, but Her Execllency who was walking on the other side of the water, in the line of fire, saw it in time and ordered him to put it away in terms more direct than have ever been addressed to a Viceroy in public.

It was in Kashmir, too, that I had my own first experience of viceregal shikar. The Maharaja had arranged a duck shoot, always the grand climax of princely entertainment during a

viceregal visit to the lovely Jhelum valley. I am an
indifferent shot, but as there was a place to spare in the
Viceroy's party I borrowed a gun and joined an ADC in the last
of the procession of boats which crept through the reeds before
first light to take up their appointed stations. Obviously the
last in the line were not expected to have much sport, perhaps
only intended to drive the birds back to the principal guns.
Hours passed and we never saw a bird, though fusillades in the
distance suggested that there were plenty.

The sun was now high and we were thirsty. A lunch basket
had been provided by our hosts, and we searched it for water,
beer or anything potable. Not a drop of liquid could we find,
except a bottle of liqueur brandy. We thought of trying the
lake water, but suspected its purity. There was nothing for it,
if we were not to perish of thirst, so we had a swig or two from
the bottle....... Suddenly the sky seemed to be full of birds.
We blazed away, shooting at everything in sight, roaring with
laughter and slapping each other on the back. We did very
little execution, but we attracted attention. Soon an emissary
from His Highness came paddling across the lake to enquire
politely what luck we had had. Clearly the Maharaja was worried
lest, by some accident, number twelve station might have upset
his careful calculations. He was no doubt relieved to hear that
our total bag at that time was two teal and a moorhen. My
companion told me that this was the occasion when I coined the
phrase 'a mallard imaginaire'.

The results of these battues were diplomatically arranged,
with due regard for protocol. At the end of the day the
slaughtered birds were laid out by hundreds in rows and counted
- but not too accurately. It was a point of courtesy that
whatever might be the size of the Viceroy's and of the
Maharaja's bag respectively, they must both be considerably
larger than anyone else's, but His Highness would be found to
have accounted for a few less than His Excellency. No one asked
for a recount.

It was in a shooting camp also - to which I was bidden, not
to shoot but to help process the continuous stream of telegrams
and despatch boxes - that I first met Jim Corbett, the legendary
shikari, who grown up with a gun in his hands in the Himalayan
foothills below his home in Naini Tal, and whose tales of
man-eating tigers in Kumaon hills are among the finest stories
ever to have made the flesh creep. He was a modest and quiet
man, a friend of the Viceroy, several of whose camps he had
helped to arrange, though he himself had long ago given up
shooting for sport.

Linlithgow had heard him tell some of his amazing
experiences and tried to persuade him to write them down.

Corbett was unwilling at first: he was not a man of letters, he seldom put pen to paper, he said. He hardly read anything but the Bible, John Bunyan and the Statesman newspaper, and he did not need the money. When the Viceroy suggested that he could devote the proceeds to St. Dunstan's, for the blind, he at last agreed, and a treasure house was unlocked.

I was standing outside my tent one evening listening to some unusually sweet bird-song when I was aware that Corbett had also come out of his tent to listen. I asked what bird it was, and he said it was the shama, the Indian nightingale. We talked about Indian birds, a subject on which Corbett was as well-informed as he was about tigers, and he invited me to join him next morning on a pad elephant, to continue the discussion.

A 'pad' elephant is saddled only with a mattress, and ours was one of several employed in driving a tiger on our last day in camp. Lady Linlithgow had to leave camp that afternoon before the rest of the party, to keep another engagement; but she wanted, before she left, to photograph a tiger with her cine-camera. A tiger was known to be in the neighbourhood, and a drive had been arranged. An ADC was to sit with Her Excellency on the machan - a platform built in a tree - with a rifle in case of accidents, and he was allowed to shoot, if there should be an opportunity after the film had been taken.

On the pad elephants we could not see what was happening, but as we approached the machans we heard a shot. the tiger had come out (we heard afterwards) and had been photographed; and the ADC had had a shot. He had hit but not killed the tiger, which had made off into the jungle.

This was a situation which Jim Corbett dreaded. He held a rapid enquiry: had the tiger turned left or right? How had it behaved? Did if fall? Roll over? Had it reared up in the air? or stumbled? He searched the ground for traces, picked up leaves and twigs, and found some blood. He was pretty sure, he said, that it had been hit in the right fore elbow.

Nothing could be done immediately as the party had to return to camp, but that afternoon another party was arranged on four elephants. A wounded tiger, a potential man-eater, could not be left in the jungle, and it must be found before sundown. It would probably lie low the first night, but by the next day it might have ranged far afield. Again Jim Corbett asked me to come with him, this time in a howdah, a kind of open box on the elephant's back. I had no rifle, but he suggested that I should bring a shot-gun with some buckshot and ball cartridges.

We went to a different part of the forest. Corbett was certain that the tiger would be lying up in one or other of two large patches of elephant grass, a mile or two distant from the events of the morning. We circled the first, more likely patch, shouting, firing guns, throwing stones. There was no result. The sun was getting low, and Corbett was anxious. 'I think we are wasting our time here' he said.

We went to the other patch of grass and repeated the performance. On our third time round we heard a low rumble, and redoubled our efforts. Suddenly Corbett touched the mahout on the shoulder, and we stopped. He turned to me and said, 'See that sapling with broad leaves? There is a fork about three feet from the ground. Put in a shot six inches below the fork'.

I could see no tiger, but did as he said. There was a thunderous roar, but no movement.

'Put in another, a few inches lower.'

I did so, and the next few seconds were full of interest. The tiger came out with a terrifying sound, straight at our elephant. The mahout - the courage of the man! - spoke one command: the elephant swayed but stood its ground. The tiger took two mighty bounds towards us, and on the third turned left through ninety degrees. As it turned Corbett fired and the tiger dropped. He put in another shot for safety, but it lay still.

We got down gingerly and examined the magnificent beast. Its right fore elbow had been shattered by the ADC's original shot. Corbett's shot, in a bad light, from the back of a swaying elephant, had probably saved many lives, and it had been the climax of an uncanny display of jungle-craft and intuition.

The quiescent stage of the war, although we did not know it, was almost at an end. In the spring of 1940 Elizabeth had to return to England, with our young son David, to go into hospital. She was still, at that time, able to travel by an Italian ship from Bombay, and by train across Europe from Genoa, but it was cutting things rather fine. Later she was convalescing at her parent's home in Jersey when the Germans drove through to the Channel Ports. She and David escaped from Jersey when the smoke from burning Cherbourg was darkening the eastern horizon. Later still they got a berth in one of the large convoys which brought civilians and troops' families to India, and they joined me in Simla in September. I was lucky.

There was an old house outside the viceregal estate which used to be occupied by married ADCs. It was said to be haunted, but not by the phantom rickshaw, which was still sometimes seen at the other end of Simla. 'Armsdell' was its name, and it had earlier been proposed to rebuild it for the use of a Deputy P.S.V. When war came it was decided to retrench on this project not by scrapping it completely but by compressing the house plan like a concertina, so that the building was barely able to accommodate the furniture which had already been made to the original measurements and now filled most of the available floor space.

We were only able to spend a few months in 'Armsdell' for soon after we moved in, the Delhi-Simla migration was discontinued except for occasional recuperative visits; but they were happy months for us, and our second son, Robin, took some of his first steps on its lawn.

We nearly lost 'Armsdell' altogether. It was on the lower slopes of an eminence known popularly as 'Snobs Hill', the upper part of which was occupied by the houses of some Members of Council. I had seen the law Member, Sir Zafrullah Khan, who had no official house of his own, casting envious eyes at 'Armsdell' as the rebuilding progressed, and I was advised to establish occupancy rights immediately by moving in to camp there as soon as the roof was on. We nearly lost it in another sense. Ghosts do not approve of their habitats being disturbed, and we were hardly installed in the new building when lightning struck a tree within a few yards of it; and soon after that the walls began to show ominous cracks which grew daily wider. Later the whole house began to slide down the hill, but that was after our time.

We did not see much of our friends in Delhi in those days. Hours of work were long, and private cars put away for shortage of petrol. We had some mobility in the daytime by harnessing David's pony to a light basket-work trap on bicycle wheels, and at night, if we went out to dinner, we might be able to hire a tonga, or we would mount a bicycle (not made for two) and proceed erratically with Elizabeth sitting on the cross-bar in front of me.

During 1940 the realities of war were still far from India. She was not yet threatened by direct attack, but the German successes in Europe and the Italian presence in North Africa made it only too clear that India and the eastern sector must plan for self-sufficiency in the event of being cut off from the West.

The Eastern Group Supply Council was set up, and Wavell's victories gave temporary relief and cheer. It may be that the Battle of Crete held up the German drive to the east for just long enough to save the defence works in the Khyber Pass from ever being put to the test.

Indian troops were acquitting themselves well, although the Congress Party had dissociated itself from the war effort, and a civil disobedience movement had been revived. In the spring of 1941 the Italians were mopped up in Abyssinia and Somaliland, and Raschid Ali's rising in Iraq was defeated. These events, nearer home to us in India than the bombing of London, were flashes of elusive victory which illumined a dark year.

In June Germany invaded Russia; in December the Japanese attacked Pearl Harbour, and we knew that in the fulness of time the fortunes of war would turn. The assurance was more intuitive than logical, for a long and bitter road backward would have to be travelled before the turning point was reached.

Meanwhile Wavell had been replaced by Auchinleck in Africa. Auchinleck was, at the time, Commander-in-Chief in India, and I was sent to convey to him personally in Simla the top-secret news of his new appointment. Wavell took command in South-East Asia, where war and defeat were to follow him inexorably.

The tide of disaster flowed up to India's shores in 1942. Singapore fell in February, and Mandalay in May. Calcutta was bombed, not severely, but enough to cause a panic evacuation. Madras was also temporarily evacuated when a Japanese task force was reported to be entering the Bay of Bengal. A 'denial' policy was put into effect in East Bengal with terrible consequences in the Bengal famine of 1943. Gandhi declared that if the Japanese arrived in India, he would submit in the spirit of non-violence, and advise Indians to do likewise. Some of his followers had more positive ideas: a general uprising was planned which would have made the Indian Mutiny, by comparison, seem like a village riot. It was forestalled by the Government's prompt action in arresting a large number of Congress leaders, but not before murder, arson and destruction of communications had been committed.

Throughout the year a succession of important visitors arrived in India. First Generalissimo and Madame Chiang Kai-shek, accompanied by Sir Archibald Clark Kerr, who had been ambassador to their court and was on his way to perform the same office at Kuibishev, which was Stalin's headquarters at that stage of the war. The purpose of the Generalissimo's visit was, apparently, to teach the Viceroy his business and to show him how the disaffected Indian leaders could be persuaded to support the war effort. In this he and his wife failed, but in the midst of their unpredictable comings and goings they had to be humoured and entertained. Gilbert Laithwaite had been struck down with pneumonia, and I had to draft the Viceroy's speech for the State Banquet in honour of his guests. This caused me to discover Confucius, whose 'Analects' I combed in translation for appropriate quotations. At the banquet itself I sat near the end of the table next to a Chinese Colonel, and I felt bound to drink level with him as he toasted me with many 'kampeis' - 'Bottoms up! like Japanese navy.' He approved of Confucius, but embarrassed me during the Generalissimo's speech in Chinese by remarking loudly,'Very bad dialect - peasant dialect.'

Hard on Chiang Kai-shek's heels came Sir Stafford Cripps,

Lord and Lady Linlithgow with Generalissimo and Madame Chiang Kai Shek in Round Garden of Viceroy's House, New Delhi, 1942

emissary of the British Cabinet, to reason and negotiate with the Indian political leaders (as yet not incarcerated) about the constitutional future. His offer was described by Gandhi as a post-dated cheque on a failing bank, and, without hindsight, there was some justification for that point of view. Not long after Sir Stafford came H.R.H. the Duke of Gloucester. I was attached to his staff as private secretary, although his was a visit with a military purpose. Other members of his staff assembled to meet Prince Henry at Karachi and we flew back with him to Delhi. As we were coming in to land we ran into a dust storm which caused our R.A.F. pilot to lose his bearings. For the best part of two hours we groped blindly and uncomfortably, a few hundred feet above the Jumna plain, trying to pick up landmarks through the haze, as our direction-finding equipment had failed. Fortunately the unmistakeable landmark of the Himalayas was spotted just in time to avoid flying into them, north of Saharanpore. Here we could identify the Jumna, and followed the river back to Delhi, to find a waiting Viceroy whose equanimity was, for once, a little disturbed.

H.R.H. and his staff covered the sub-continent in enormous bounds, by air, rail and road: from Peshawar and the Khyber Pass to Ranchi in the east, from Delhi to Bangalore, and further to Ceylon, which had recently had an unpleasant taste of Japanese carrier-borne aircraft. The main object was to visit military centres and troops who had come out of Burma, or were preparing to return to fight there. In the course of Prince Henry's travels he was bound to come in contact with the civil and political side of Indian affairs, and my function was to be at hand for any information or guidance that might be required in that context. His physical energy and concentration were remarkable, throughout the long, hot or drenching monsoon days, filled with inspections of troops and visits to establishments, and far into the nights and small hours; but like Linlithgow, he only completely relaxed in the intimate circle of his own staff.

He had to deliver a nation-wide broadcast speech while he was in Delhi, and there was a moment of panic when, shortly before he was to go on the air, H.R.H. was not to be found. I ran him to earth, with three minutes to spare, in a state of royal undress. He had been in the swimming pool, and had just poured himself a whisky and soda.

'Can I come as I am? Can I bring this with me?'

'You've hardly time to drink it now, sir.'

We made our way to the nether regions of Viceroy's House. Mr. A.S. Bokhari, Director of All-India Radio, dressed hotly for the occasion in morning coat and stock, stared at the figure in unbelted bush-shirt and sandals, with tousled hair, and then, with eyebrows raised in a wild surmise, looked at me, following behind, for confirmation that this was the royal visitor.

Prince Henry, still carrying his whisky, gulped it down and delivered the broadcast with great panache.

'I must remember that when I have to speak again' I overheard him say to himself as we came away.

On the evening before H.R.H. left India from Karachi, his equerry, Howard Kerr, came up to me. 'You are going to have an honour conferred upon you' he said. I wondered what it would be. Surely I had not done enough to earn even a third class M.V.O.

'You are going to be ducked by Prince Henry in the pool tonight. It's a mark of favour. He doesn't do it to many people. There are just some simple rules to be observed. H.R.H. will come to bathe at about six-thiry: you should enter the water at six-twenty-five, and paddle about aimlessly in the middle. When you hear a great splashing behind you, do not look round. You will then be ducked, several times; but on no account must you try to retaliate.'

And so it befell, and my honourable discomfiture was enjoyed by all.

I joined the Delhi Light Horse, the local Auxiliary Force unit, for exercise, for good company and because I liked horses. We paraded in the cold misty mornings under the walls of the Red Fort. We trotted and cantered, knee to knee, jingle of harness and spurs, good smell of saddle soap and horse sweat. 'Half sections, left wheel! Sections, right into line! Form column of sections, left! Sections, about! Troop, halt!' One could do it half asleep, except when, under the eye of our troop sergeant-instructor, we had to go over the jumps, demolishing dummy enemies with our swords.

When the Japanese were approaching India, the Delhi Light Horse were given an operational role. Our training was concentrated on the defence of the Willingdon airport from a possible airborne attack. We came to know every fold of ground, nullah, bush and rock in the rough country surrounding the airport. Once, in the middle of an exercise, we saw a solitary horseman approaching us. It turned out to be General Wavell, at that time Commander-in-Chief in India, who was out for his morning ride. He asked some questions, told us to carry on and watched our manoeuvres with interest for a while. As he left us he remarked, 'Well, I've learned something this morning: I didn't know I still had any mounted troops under my command.'

The Delhi Light Horse were only once, while I served with them, called out and embodied for action: and that was during the emergency following the arrest of the Congress leaders in

1942, when for a few days there were serious civil disturbances. I was given special leave of absence from the Private Secretary's office. We patrolled the streets of Delhi, and bivouacked at night in Connaught Circus, sleeping on the ground with saddles as our pillows. My viceregal khitmutgar could not bear the thought that I was roughing it within half a mile of him, and every evening, resplendent in scarlet and gold, came to find me, bearing a tray of drinks.

Early in 1943 a new Department of Food was being assembled to deal with the increasing problem of army and civilian supply, which included the possibility of local shortages in Bengal and southern India. I applied to join the new department, but left the Viceroy's staff with real regret. When I took leave of Lord Linlithgow we walked up and down his garden, and he spoke of the matter which lay heavy on his mind at that time. Gandhi, then under detention, had declared a hunger fast and had already gone without food for ten days. He was beginning to show signs of failing and, at the age of seventy-four, whether he intended to die or not, nature might take control. Indian Members of Council had resigned and Sir Maurice Gwyer, Chief Justice of India, a deeply sincere and respected man, had implored the Viceroy to release the Mahatma and not to risk having the blood of a saint on his head. But Linlithgow, who thought much about his own health from time to time, had also informed himself carefully about Gandhi's physical metabolism by consulting doctors who had attended the Mahatma and knew his constitution. He had his own views of Gandhi's method of negotiation. He believed that there was no serious risk of his dying, and was determined not to yield to this form of blackmail. With great moral courage he held out against all the pressures, and was justified in the event. The fast was ended after twenty-one days and, miraculously, in the last few days before he called it off, the Mahatma had actually gained some weight.

There ought to be a statue to Lord Linlithgow. Sir Edwin Lutyens, on the look-out for a commission, remarked that there had never been an equestrian statue of a viceroy, and asked whether he might have the honour of designing one of Linlithgow. The Viceroy replied that horsemanship did not come so naturally to him as to justify that distinction; but what about showing him astride a bull? He was proud of his contribution to the improvement of India's cattle by the introduction of stud bulls. But perhaps not; for if he were to be shown riding a bull, was there not a risk that he might be mistaken for Europa?

Lutyens was not amused. It was a pity. Lord Linlithgow, mounted on a bull, and aiming a catapult, would have looked well at the entrance to the Agricultural Institute at Pusa; and it would undoubtedly have qualified him in due course to enter the Hindu pantheon.

6

Last Post and Morning Drum

For those who were serving in India during the last five years of British rule the experience was not unlike that of runners in the last stages of a long-distance race. The earlier stages may have been exhilarating, but the last lap, which will end with triumph or disappointment, inevitably has its grim moments.

During four of those five years, India's troubles were a small part of the world conflagration; but they were enough to provide material for melodrama on a continental scale — revolutionary politics, bitter civil and religious strife, mass murder, famine and, on the eastern frontiers, an enemy invasion. This last was halted and then repelled by a defence as desperate and heroic as any in history, when defeat and retreat were turned into victory, and India's Thermopylae was fought, and won, by British and Indian troops on Garrison Hill at Kohima.

Civil officers in Delhi, like myself, were far removed from most of the strife; but of the final scene which was enacted in Delhi, and in which I had a walking-on part, and of a tragic interlude before it, I can give some account. I had left Lord Linlithgow's staff in February, 1943 to join the Food Department of the Government of India.

I wonder how many people remember, or have even heard of, the Bengal famine of 1943? It would not be surprising if they were few, outside Bengal; for while the famine was at its height the war was also reaching its climax on every front, on land and sea and in the air. Yet over a million people died of starvation in that year, in five districts of Bengal alone, and many more from the diseases of malnutrition which followed in its wake. It was almost entirely a man made famine, a major disaster of war.

In the summer of 1942 the Japanese were expected to attempt an invasion of India by land and sea, in preparation for which a scorched earth policy was carried out - if that term can be applied to a region which is mostly water, silt and mangrove swamp - a denial policy over the coastal area of eastern Bengal. For many miles inland, villages were evacuated, stocks of food and cattle removed and boats, almost the only means of communication, were systematically destroyed.

Over the centuries there have been serious famines in India, for most of the people lived at subsistence level, and in a normal year there was only just enough food to go round. The famines were nearly always local, and they occurred when some natural calamity, drought or flood, had caused a greater shortage than could be covered by food moving, in the course of trade, from areas of plenty to areas of scarcity.

There were over seven hundred thousand villages in India before partition, and over most of the country, even after the railways were built, transport of goods between them was by head load or bullock cart along a network of village paths, (sometimes impassable in the monsoon), or by boat in the river areas. Since the range and capacity of a bullock-cart are limited by its slow daily rate of progress and by the amount of food which the bullocks themselves consume, the boat-served areas were usually better off for food supplies.

As communications improved famines became less frequent, and the provisions of the Famine Code were applied as soon as a threat of scarcity appeared in any part of the country. The Famine Code usually forestalled a famine. Public works were ordered, the building of roads or embankments, the digging or repair of tanks; and the villagers of the affected area who were employed to do the work were fed, or earned enough to buy food.

In 1942 the war was approaching India at the speed of a cyclone. East Bengal, now Bangladesh, is one of the most densely populated parts of the world. The staple food of the people is rice and a little fish; and because of the ease of inter-village communication by innumerable waterways, serious scarcity was comparatively unknown. Some special kinds of rice used even to be exported, but Bengal was marginally a net importer of rice from Burma and Siam, sources of supply which were no longer available.

The main rice crop in Bengal is harvested in the winter, but because of the denial policy, that harvest was short in the southern districts of East Bengal in the winter of 1942. The people could have been fed from the surplus elsewhere, if it had reached them in time. Statistically there was enough food in India, even in Bengal itself, to have prevented starvation in East Bengal, but the fear which turns a shortage into famine takes no account of statistics. The danger signals were not overlooked; they were under-estimated. The Government of India's responsibility was to ensure that the armed forces were fed; that of the provincial governments was to plan and provide for the feeding of their people.

In parts of Bengal, and particularly in the south-east,

cultivation is done mainly by a large class of landless labourers, paid partly or wholly in kind by the landlords who are usually small farmers. The purchase of rice for the army combined with the short crop in the south caused the local price of grain to rise, and people began to hoard. The landlords soon decided to keep the grain or sell it, and pay their labourers in cash, but as paddy disappeared and prices rose, the cash was not enough to feed them.

Panic grows silently and swiftly. So remote were the areas at first affected that few, even in Bengal itself, knew what was happening. The first reports of distress reached Delhi in March of 1943, but there had been a state of famine for some weeks before that. By the time it was acknowledged, it was beyond control and too late to halt the tragedy. The menfolk of thousands of villages left home to find work and food elsewhere; no doubt they intended to return, but few of them did. Their wives and children and the old folk starved.

The terrible infection of fear began to spread. Soon emaciated figures began to haunt the outskirts of Calcutta. Feeding centres were set up; soldiers offered to the starving their bread or chupatties, but to Bengalis this was unfamiliar food from which many turned in disgust, and died. The Press, with the best intentions, proclaimed and photographed the horror, but this did little more than aggravate it, and enlarge the areas of fear and avarice and hoarding.

It was a disastrous year, but bountiful heaven brought relief with the autumn crop, and a bumper harvest in the winter. By that time, too, large-scale procurement of grain had been organised, and the army, its battle for India won and the Japanese in retreat, was able to lend a hand in the distribution.

After the rescue operation - the losing battle to save lives and relieve the immediate impact of the famine - we could turn in 1944 and the following years to something more constructive. A nucleus of the Food Department had been formed early in 1943 to regulate food supplies for the army and the civil population, not to meet the emergency of famine. It developed, with its counterparts in the Provinces and States, into a large combined operation manned by soldiers and civilians, merchants and officials, retired generals and judges. During the desperate months in which the utmost human effort seemed only a drop in the ocean of what needed to be done, these varied elements were fused into an amalgam of skills and experience which was able to accomplish much of lasting value in the ensuing years.

There were parts of India potentially as vulnerable as Bengal; north Bihar, liable to devastating floods; dry zones

in the south Deccan and the thickly populated coastal strip of
Travancore and Cochin. There were other areas comfortably
surplus in wheat and rice; wide, irrigated prairies in the
Punjab and the Indus valley of Sind. But in hoarding supplies
governments can be as selfish as individuals, and it took much
hard bargaining and heated argument for the Central Government
to organise a system of controlled procurement and distribution.
Rationing was introduced in the main cities: some governments
and their officials protested loudly, but eventually operated
the unfamiliar regime with great efficiency.

Indians do not take easily to controls which are not a part
of their own social obligations; and they are more particular
about their food than most people, mainly on religious grounds.
Hindu widows in some parts would sooner die than eat milled
rice; for them it must be hand-pounded. Certain faddists would
eat nothing but parboiled grain; others must have it polished.
Barley excoriated the stomachs of some; millet reduced the
social status of others. All this complicated the difficuties
of food supply.

Storage was a problem. There were no grain silos, even at
the ports. Most Indian village households store their grain in
straw bins, or underground. In innumerable markets great and
small, there were ramshackle sheds in which sacks of grain lay
in disorderly heaps, and often they were stacked out of doors.
Hundreds of thousands of tons of grain were lost every year from
the depredations of rats, weevils and the damp. With the help
of army engineers we improvised prefabricated sheds for
immediate use, and had to teach the art of stacking bagged
grain. Then we planned for more permanent storage, choosing
carefully where the depots should be built, in both surplus and
deficit areas, and bearing in mind that the sight of stored
grain reserves can stop the ebb of confidence which is often the
cause of famine.

Grain storage was, for a time, my own special
responsibility, working alongside a distinguished 'sapper'
general, lately Engineer-in-Chief, Sir Clarence Bird. I was
temporarily in charge of the Food Department for a few weeks,
after the Secretary, Major-General Ernest Wood had been sent
urgently to the North-East frontier to organise the evacuation
of refugees from Burma; and I later acted as Director-General
until relieved by Dr. B.R. Sen, a senior Bengali officer who,
for many years after the war, was head of the Food and
Agriculture Organisation of the United Nations.

We combined with the Department of Agriculture to promote a
'grow more food' campaign throughout India, which seemed, at the
time, to make painfully slow progress. This was hardly
surprising as all the good arable land in India had been

The Food Department, under Lieutenant General Sir Clarence Bird, Lahore, 1946

cultivated for centuries; only marginally fertile new land could be brought under the plough, and this was watered by an uncertain rainfall. The farmer let his scrub cattle and his goats eat his firewood, and burned the fertilising farmyard manure as fuel. He saw no sense in paying taxes to meet the cost of tube-well irrigation, or in buying unfamiliar chemicals to put on his land. The implements and seed his great-grandfather had used were good enough for him. But now, nearly forty years after we began our war-time drive to enlarge the area and improve the method of food production, we hear reports of a 'green revolution' in India. Forty years is a short period in history. Perhaps, after all, our labours had not been in vain.

My family used to go for the summer months to Kashmir, where our elder son was at school and where I was able to join them for short holidays. Once we were in a house-boat by Nagin Bagh, on a part of the Dal Lake, and once in a hut among high-piled snowdrifts in Gulmarg, a lovely alp, starred with gentians and wild tulips. The first sight of the vale of Kashmir, whether approached from Jammu through the road tunnel at the top of the Banihal pass, or from Rawalpindi through the Jhelum gorge, is an unforgettable experience, having something of the quality of a mystical initiation, the emotional impact of sudden contrast. After climbing for hours from the scorched, dusty plain, one bursts through a rocky barrier into an unbelievable vision. At one's feet stretches a temperate valley where, in spring, the almond and apricot trees are in blossom and the water-meadows are carpeted with a dwarf blue iris; and in autumn the land glows with the pale gold of poplars and the red gold of chenar trees. Above all is a turquoise sky and the ring of snow peaks in the distance. So sharp was the contrast with war and famine, that these brief glimpses of paradise had the unreality of a dream.

In 1946 I had some home leave, the first for nine years. London was battered and war-weary, but it was good to see. We spent much of the leave in Jersey, where Elizabeth's parents had remained throughout the enemy occupation. They had the ultimate satisfaction of receiving the surrender of seventeen German panzers which had been stabled on their property, when their commander could find no other authority to relieve him of his charge.

Before my leave was over I was ordered to Copenhagen to be Secretary of the Indian delegation to the United Nations F.A.O. Conference. My recollection of this is of an amount of speech-making and reciprocal entertainment disproportionate to the results achieved, and also of a good deal of political infighting among the mixed assortment of Indian representatives.

One member, an enormous Pathan from the North-West Frontier Province, Abdul Ghani Khan, wrote about the Conference later, and described my own functions as 'enquiry office, complaint register, money exchange, travel bureau, law and order and finance department rolled into one'. It was interesting, but it all seemed rather irrelevant to the food problems of India at that time.

We returned to India in October. By this time the Viceroy, Lord Wavell, had reconstructed his Council by inviting Congress and Moslem League nominees to form a provisional government, and there was a new Member of Council in charge of Food Department, Dr. Rajendra Prasad, who later became the first President of the Republic of India. But I had hardly made his acquaintance when I was removed from his jurisdiction.

An urgent and, in the circumstances, surprising message from Viceroy's House to the Department required that I should be relieved of my duties at once, in order to take up a new post of Joint Private Secretary on the Viceroy's staff. Surprising because such changes are not usually made at very short notice; and George Abell, the Private Secretary, who had taken over from me as Deputy P.S.V. four years before, already had a full complement of staff and, although undoubtedly hard-worked, was in good health and heart, and seemed not particularly in need of my assistance. There is more in this than meets the eye, I thought, and there was.

For two years or so Lord Wavell had been striving patiently to bring Congress and the Moslem League together, to co-operate in provisional arrangements for government at the Centre, pending a constitutional settlement under which the British power could be transferred to the government of a united India. He had succeeded to the point of forming a government containing representatives of both major political parties, with Jawaharlal Nehru as Chief Minister. It had not worked well; co-operation did not extend to agreement about a Constituent Assembly, and the real party leaders on each side, Gandhi and Jinnah, had not been helpful. Jinnah was already committed to an independent Pakistan, anathema to Gandhi, and both realised that the way to gain their irreconcilable ends was not to be drawn an inch forward by compromise, but rather to lean further and further back.

Wavell was tired, and could make no progress. He was liked and trusted by all: except for the murderous Calcutta riots in August 1946, he had managed, more or less, to keep the peace between Hindus and Moslems: he had maintained the political dialogue, but he lacked the flair, the zest and perhaps the imagination to break the deadlock.

Towards the end of 1946 he had returned to London for

discussions with Mr. Attlee and his Cabinet. In the course of these Wavell had made a proposal which reflected the soldier's mind: it was, to concentrate the civil and military resources of the Government, to retire to new positions and to hold them for as long as might be necessary. The Indian army and the Indian members, Hindu and Moslem, of the civil services, including the subordinate services who turned the wheels of government, still showed amazing loyalty, although they must soon begin to look over their shoulders at shadows which were rapidly overtaking them. There were fewer British troops at that time in the whole of India than there were in Palestine, a country about as large as a fair-sized Indian district.

Wavell's proposal was that, in India south of the Ganges valley and the Indus delta, power should be transferred to a Congress government or governments. The population of that area was almost entirely Hindu. Other communities were in such a small minority that they could hardly pose a communal problem. In the Indus and Ganges valleys, including Bengal, where the communities were more evenly divided, the Government of India should concentrate its civil and military strength, and hold the fort until a settlement could be reached.

He made a stipulation. Such an arrangement might well be accompanied by a serious disturbances. No one could foretell what form they would take or against whom they would be directed; but it was not unlikely that the lives of some forty thousand British civilians in India, and of other loyal citizens, would be in danger. Preparations should be made for their protection, and if necessary for the evacuation from India of the women and children.

Mr. Attlee's Government decided that, in the matter of transfer of power, large though the cherry was, they should not take two bites at it. Lord Wavell was allowed to return to India without an answer to his proposal. It was agreed, however, that he should prepare secretly the security precautions which he had suggested. Attlee had, in fact, already decided that Lord Wavell must be replaced, and his choice for the replacement had fallen on Lord Mountbatten, formerly Supreme Allied Commander in South East Asia, with the laurels of Burma and the Japanese surrender fresh upon him.

It was a brilliant choice, but the manner of Lord Wavell's dismissal was not happy. Although the decision had been made before January, Wavell was not told about it until mid-February and was given a very short time to leave. Arrangements had been made for his daughter's wedding in New Delhi in February, and Wavell asked for and was granted a short postponement of the announcement of his supersession. Meanwhile the plan for the evacuation of civilians in an emergency was to be put in hand –

and this is where I came in.

A very senior officer who had recently left India on retirement was chosen for the task; but he could not return immediately (and in fact he never came). I was to make a start on the planning, and, because of the need for secrecy, I had to work under the cover of an innocent-seeming appointment. Since the war in the east was at last finished, it was only to be expected that the next few Indian honours lists would be longer than usual. Normally the P.S.V. would have been able without difficulty to handle the extra work involved, but with more urgent constitutional work on his hands, what could be more natural than that a newly-appointed member of the Viceroy's staff should relieve him of it? I was made secretary of the Honours Committee, and this accounted for the Joint Private Secretary's frequent consultations in New Delhi with senior officers of all the services, and for his travels over India for discussions with Governors and officials in the provinces. It was a thin cover, but I doubt if anyone outside the secret took any interest in my goings on.

The plan on which I was really engaged was one which, because of the incalculable factors, was not likely to have worked out as intended, but the framework had to be constructed; and within six weeks, by the time Lord Mountbatten arrived, the framework, although not all the detail, was complete.

Emergency plans for concentration, which already existed in every city, district and sub-division, were brought up to date; camps and depots were earmarked and arrangements made for stocking them with food, clothing, medicines and other necessities; transport and escorts were arranged. All had to be done without attracting attention. I was an especial thorn in the flesh of the Quarter-Master Gereral's branch of Army headquarters, as the Commander-in-Chief, Sir Claude Auchinleck, later had occasion to point out to me; but I had all the co-operation I dared to expect, from busy men for a contingency plan.

Lord Wavell, naturally took an interest in what I was doing: I reported to him from time to time, but was allowed to get on with the work without interruption. Wavell's awkward silences could sometimes be formidable, but I did not experience them when I came to report progress. He used to describe similar plans which he had caused to be prepared in Egypt during the war, and demonstrated with the aid of ink-pots and paper-weights on his desk.

When the time for his departure was near, Lord Wavell gave a private dinner party for his staff and their wives. With a wry sense of humour and twinkle in his only eye, he touched on the recent events. He compared himself to King Nebuchadnezzar,

'who, as you remember, heard a voice from heaven, the equivalent
in those days, I suppose, of a telegram from Whitehall. Some
lines, which could be appropriate to my own case, came into my
head:

> The banished monarch, now put out to grass
> with patient oxen and the humble ass,
> said, as he champed the unaccustomed food,
> 'It may be wholesome, but it is not good'

Lord Mountbatten was bringing his own staff with him,
including several naval and military officers who had been with
him in the South-East Asia Command - among them was Ronald
Brockman, then and afterwards for many years his Private
Secretary. Lord Wavell's staff, however, were told to stay at
their posts until the new Viceroy had a look at them. He spoke
to each of us about our duties, and when he came to me he said,
'Planning an evacuation, are you? That's not my idea at all. I
shall have to think about you. But you may as well finish off
what you are doing now. Meanwhile report to Pug Ismay; no
doubt he'll give you plenty of other things to do.'

And so it turned out. We all stayed and pulled happily and
hard together in double harness, the old and the new staff, for
the most memorable and exciting one hundred and forty-five days
of our lives.

Mountbatten had also brought with him two doughty
supporters, General Lord Ismay, who had been Winston Churchill's
Chief of Staff, and Sir Eric Mieville, who had been a Private
Secretary to the King. Viceroy's House was familiar territory
to them both, for they had once served together there, in an
earlier regime, as Military Secretary and Private Secretary
respectively.

Of the Viceroy himself and of his lady, Edwina, one cannot
write except in superlatives, and one burst of superlatives must
suffice for each. For those who served with him at that time
Lord Mountbatten was not only everything that history had
recorded and will record of him, brilliant, inspiring,
courageous, tireless; he was also a great leader, the perfect
commanding officer. He drove his staff hard, but never harder
than he drove himself, and whatever he asked one to do, it was
as if he conferred a favour. At the end of the short time that
I was privileged to work with him, I would have followed him
anywhere.

Lady Mountbatten was the perfect partner for such a man, at
such a time. Her energy matched his; she found her own work to
do in India, and never did she encroach upon his sphere or stand
in his limelight. In all that they did, they complemented each
other. No wonder that they achieved what had seemed almost

Lord Mountbatten and Lord Ismay in Parliament Buildings, New Delhi, 1947

impossible, and in less than half the allotted time.

The speed of events and the variety of problems that followed each other in rapid succession could easily have produced an impression of tumult and confusion in the Viceroy's camp; in fact a basic order prevailed throughout all the activity, each man understanding, however varied his duties might be, exactly what was expected of him at any given time, and how it would fit in to the general scheme. An example of the mechanism which helped to achieve this was the staff conference, which began each working day.

Generally about twelve of us attended. There was no agenda; Mountbatten would first recount, with penetrating and amusing comment, what had happened the day before, and what was likely to arise that day. Widely differing subjects were raised and dissected; we all took part and spoke our minds, for it was clearly understood that we were expected to have views of our own, and that yes-men were not welcome. Ideas popped out of His Excellency's head like rabbits out of a warren, and it was the duty of his staff to catch them, and return the wilder ones to their holes before they had run too far.

The whole discussion, however much the strands crossed, overlapped or went off at a tangent, was taken down in patient long-hand by Vernon Erskine Crum, the conference secretary, a young soldier with a fine war record, and an extraordinary talent for straightening out in the minutes the tangled skein of debate and decision. He was a splendid secretary, who could have been excused for spending long hours,

'racking his brains to record and report what he thinks
they will think that they ought to have thought'

In fact he produced the results, lucidly arranged, with exemplary speed.

Lord Ismay, with whom most of my own work was done, was a revelation. One had the impression, at first, of a simple soldier (unlike Mountbatten, whom no one could have mistaken for a simple sailor), but in fact he had an acute and tenacious mind, and the kind of genius which is a combination of inexorable commonsense with the taking of infinite pains.

He also had a gift for handling people. He was invaluable to H.E. not only as a trouble-shooter, but as a pourer of oil on troubled waters, a conciliator when clashes of temperament or character were holding up progress in any direction. This gift would be exercised not only on the high and great, but in the interest of humbler objects like myself.

'What have you been doing to Claude Auchinleck?' he asked me one day. 'He's got some painful corns, you know: you mustn't tread on them.' There had been a thunderous protest from the Commander-in-Chief's house that I had been bullying the Q.M.G's officers to earmark army transport for my evacuation plans. 'Come on; we'll go and see him'.

The Field-Marshal was in a towering rage, flanked by the Q.M.G. himself, General Sir Ernest Wood, an old colleague of mine in the Food Department. In half an hour's discussion, during which Ismay never wavered for a moment in loyalty to his subordinate, the matter was sorted out. As we went downstairs, Auchinleck (that great man) clapped me on the shoulder. 'You mustn't mind me', he said, 'my bark's worse than my bite.'

His Majesty's Government had already announced, at the time of Lord Mountbatten's appointment, that June 1948 was the target date for the transfer of power to an Indian government. The Viceroy was determined to advance that date if he possibly could, for two reasons. The first because there was a real doubt (justified by subsequent events in the Punjab) whether the resources available to maintain law and order could take the strain for so long, or could prevent a conflagration which would have indefinitely postponed an orderly transfer. The second was Mountbatten's own technique for accelerating the tempo of progress towards agreement, by consolidating a point of negotiation as soon as it was gained and allowing the parties no time to have second thoughts.

The objective was still to hand over power to the government of a united India. In all the cut and thrust of negotiation to this end, it became apparent to some of us that partition, before the word had been officially breathed or its possibility openly admitted (at any rate in the Viceroy's camp) was likely, however unpalatable, to be the solution. At a private lunch in the house of V.P. Menon, the constitutional adviser, six of us discussed the implications and decided that, since it is the duty of civil servants to protect their masters from being taken by surprise, we must have ready for the Viceroy a contingent plan which could be laid before the political leaders, if and when they should decide to cut their Gordian Knot.

The plan would set out what would be involved in dividing the assets and liabilities of India, from rolling stock to currency reserves, from the national debt to the armed forces; and it would make proposals for carrying out the division. It should avoid making the process seem too formidable, but would try to show the leaders that, before partition could be effective, there was much hard work to be done, and not a moment to be lost in getting down to it.

I was asked to undertake this task, with the help - if I

could get it - of two other I.C.S. officers, H.M. Patel and Chaudhuri Mohammed Ali, Hindu and Moslem respectively and both well known to me. Mohammed Ali was later to be Prime Minister of Pakistan. I let them into the secret, and we had a series of lunch-time meetings, à trois in my house, at which the plan was hammered out and began to take shape. They did most of the hard work; I did the editing, reconciliation and stitching together. Reconciliation in another sense was sometimes necessary, for the bargaining was tough and on several occasions a 'walk-out' by one or other of my colleagues was narrowly averted. Thus came about the paper known as 'The Administrative Consequences of Partition'.

At length the plan was complete, or as complete as it could be. It was not intended to be more than a plan in outline, but it turned out to be a fairly voluminous example of what is nowadays called a pre-feasibility study.

When, on June 3rd, the political leaders accepted the inevitability of the British Government's decision to divide and quit - or rather, to give them the option to divide - the Viceroy threw down 'The Administrative Consequences' onto the table with dramatic effect. 'Now, gentlemen' he said, 'this is what partition means. This is the job we must get down to at once, and finish before the fifteenth of August.'

The work of Patel and Mohammed Ali had only just begun. They became a steering committee of the Partition Council under the Viceroy, to put the plan into effect. The fact that the transfer of power could take place on the date announced was due to the devoted and unflagging labour and co-operation of those two men during the next ten weeks. If the will to co-operate had continued beyond that date, much bloodshed and unhappiness might have been avoided.

On the day after the decision was announced, a tear-off calendar appeared on every official's desk: '70 days left to prepare for Transfer of Power' - and so on, in diminishing sequence.

Patel and Mohammed Ali worked on. Every night I waited in my office until the fruit of their day's labour was brought in, twenty or thirty files, each dealing with a subject arising out of the enormous and complex problem of division. In the rare cases when they had not been able to agree on their recommendation, I made my own and sent the files to the Viceroy, sometimes not before midnight.

Occasionally my telephone would ring early in the morning, and Mountbatten would summon me to discuss some point. He would be in bed, with files all over it and on the floor. Her Excellency might be sitting at her dressing table. Once there was certainly a mongoose playing in the room - I cannot have

dreamed it - perhaps Pamela Mountbatten had brought it in.   By
nine o'clock H.E. was ready to announce to the Partition Council
the progress made, and obtain their endorsement.

Another job which I had in those days was a different kind
of evacuation plan, not so secret.   After six years of war there
was a long waiting list of British and other civilians and their
families, for passages to Europe on ships which were in short
supply.   Their needs competed with those of others, of army
families and of special categories, such as Polish refugees who
had made their escape overland to India, where they had spent
the duration of the war.   All these urgencies had to be
co-ordinated, and the arrival of passengers at the quayside so
timed that not a square foot of scarce shipping space was
avoidably wasted.   I took a hand in this complicated process,
and also had to see that H.E's voice was heard from time to time
above the clamour for ships from many corners of the world.

Elizabeth and I also had to think about our own future.   I
would soon be forty-two, with a family to educate, and that was
not the best age for changing jobs.   We were both inclined to
stay in India for a few more years.   The Indian Government,
which would have at its disposal a number of very able senior
Indian officers, was lukewarm in its invitation to British
officers to remain in its service after Independence.   Pakistan,
which would not be so well equipped administratively, seemed to
welcome foreign mercenaries, civil and military, more warmly.
We had many friends among both Hindu and Moslem officers in the
Services;   but, rightly or wrongly, we felt that, since neither
country would be denuded of experience, we might before long
find that we were overstaying our welcome if we remained in the
service of either of the new governments.

I   therefore applied to appear before the selection
committee which the Home Government had set up to pick whatever
they could use out of the soon-to-be-disbanded Indian Civil
Service.   In July I was allowed for this purpose seven days
leave from door to door, packed a toothbrush and climbed into an
aeroplane for London.

The Selection Committee were kind, and offered me a post in
the Foreign Service.   In fact I was told that, if I could make
up my mind quickly, I would be posted Deputy High Commissioner
in Lahore.   I was tempted to accept the offer at once, but I
asked for some days' grace to talk it over with my wife.   I was
on the point of leaving London to return to India, when a cable
arrived telling me to stay where I was and await the arrival of
Lord Ismay at the India Office.   A knotty problem had arisen.
It had earlier been agreed - or so it was thought - that
Mountbatten would stay on after Independence as Governor-General
of both India and Pakistan, with Jawaharlal Nehru and Mohammed

Ali Jinnah as Prime Ministers repectively of the two countries.
Then Jinnah had second thoughts: he would prefer to be supreme
head in his own state.   Nehru wished Mountbatten to stay on in
India in any case, but H.E. himself was doubtful.   This was an
unexpected turn of events on which the British Cabinet must be
consulted.

Lord Ismay arrived, and put the question to Mr. Attlee, who
was   inclined   to   let   Mountbatten   remain   for   a   period   as
Governor-General of India only;   but he asked Ismay to sound the
views of leaders of the Opposition.   Ismay saw Harold Macmillan
and others,   and   then   went   down   to   see   Winston   Churchill   at
Chartwell.   He described the scene to me when he returned to
London that evening.

When he had taken leave of his old wartime master, four
months before, Churchill had addressed him, with tears streaming
down his face: 'Pug, I love you very much;   but I hate the
thought of what you have chosen to do.   You will fail in your
endeavour, I have no doubt at all.   And, mark my words, when you
return to this country, having failed, I shall not hesitate to
impeach you.'

When Ismay arrived at Chartwell this time, he found Mr.
Churchill in the garden.   He stopped some yards away from him
and said, 'I wonder if I am an unwelcome visitor, sir.'

'Hullo, Pug,' said Churchill.   'Not so;   far from it.   I am
very glad to see you again.   Things seem to be going better than
I had supposed.   Come along in.   Tell me all about it.'

Ismay brought back with him a message from the Leader of
the Opposition, a single sheet of note paper inscribed by
Churchillian hand in Churchillian prose, to the effect that he
entirely approved the proposal that Mountbatten should stay on
as Governor-General of India.

The next evening Ismay asked me to go along to 10 Downing
Street with him, to attend a Cabinet Committe meeting.   I
watched with admiration Mr. Attlee's conduct of that meeting.
He was the perfect chairman.   On the main subject the discussion
was unexpectedly long, but the Prime Minister steered it
skilfully and, at the end, pushed back his chair, closed his
eyes and summed up, in words which I heard him repeat, almost
verbatim, when he spoke in the debate on the India Independence
Bill in the House of Commons some days later.

Then I was invited to pour out my small beer, about ships
for India.   This was sympathetically received, and I was
referred to another committee, composed mainly of high-powered
soldiers and sailors, which met on the next day in a bomb-proof
subterranean office beneath Whitehall.

When Ismay's party returned to India, it included a British

major, expert on Sikh affairs, to advise the Viceroy on the handling of that vigorous minority which would be cruelly split by partition. This man had named a stiffish price for his services, and I had been bidden in London to call on the Treasury and persuade them to pick up the bill, as for some reason Mountbatten did not wish it to be a charge on Indian revenues. I was armed with a personal letter of approval from the Prime Minister, but was told not to play this card unless I had to.

I forget whom I saw, but they were two very senior and hard-faced men. Not unexpectedly, they turned me down flat. Then I presented Mr. Attlee's letter, feeling like, and no doubt regarded as a card-sharper who produces an ace from his sleeve. I have avoided re-entering the Treasury Building since that day.

We travelled back to India in an R.A.F. plane, with over-night stops at Malta and Habbaniyeh. In Delhi we found that the race for Independence had entered the final straight.

The partition of India involved, by the decision of provincial legislatures voting in communal sections, the partition also of two Moslem majority provinces, Bengal and Punjab, both of which had large areas in which Hindus (or Sikhs) were locally more numerous. The difficult task of drawing a boundary line which would apportion Hindu and Moslem areas respectively to the appropriate country, was entrusted to a Boundary Commission in which the communities were equally represented, and of which the chairman was a distinguished British lawyer, Sir Cyril Radcliffe. As his colleagues almost invariably disagreed, most of the decisions had to be taken by the chairman himself. This was a blessing in disguise because it had the effect of delaying the publication of the Commission's report until after the dates fixed for the two Independence Days, so that the celebration of those Days should not be clouded by the inevitable discontents to which the boundary award would give rise.

As the Viceroy could not be in two places at once to preside over the transfer of power to the new dominions, it was decided that Independence Day in Karachi would be on 14th August and in Delhi on the 15th. The question of H.E.'s speeches for the two occasions had been somehow overlooked until rather late. Mountbatten was a good extempore speaker, but he had not had much opportunity or inclination, in the crowded days since he had arrived in India, to deliver set speeches. It was felt by his staff that the formality of the Independence Days ceremonial called for prepared speeches. I was told to draft one for the Viceroy to deliver in Karachi - and to be quick about it.

I had not done this sort of thing for years, and was out of practice. My wartime efforts for Lord Linlithgow had been influenced by Winston Churchill's style, which somehow would not be quite appropriate in the mouth of Lord Mountbatten. I lacked Gilbert Laithwaite's gift of being able faithfully to render his master's thoughts and words. Understandably, therefore, when Mountbatten was presented with the fait accompli of my draft at the next staff meeting, he complained that 'this may be alright for John Christie, but it isn't me!' Quite true, but there was no time to rewrite it, or do more than make a few alterations; and Pakistan received her Independence to the accompaniment of, at any rate, some of my resounding phrases.

One of them referred to the history that was being made that day, and drew some rather obvious comparisons of history to a river, that sometimes moved with the slowness of a glacier, and at other times in spate - 'We who are making history today are caught and carried on in the swift current of events; there is no time to look back - there is time only to look forward.'

I was gratified later to find that Lord Mountbatten had, in more leisurely retrospect, so far identified himself with this sentiment as to choose for the title of a collection of his speeches: 'Time only to look forward'.

Nothing marred the rejoicing and triumph of those two days in the capital cities. There was a lull in the communal ferocity, though its blood-lust was far from satisfied yet. If, for some Congress Party and Moslem League politicians, it was the end of a war of independence, no struggle had ended with more demonstration of friendship and mutual congratulation between the transferor and the transferees of power. The friendship between Britain and the two successor States has persisted, with ups and downs, for thirty five years. It was then too early, perhaps it is still too early, for congratulation.

I had no official part in the celebrations, for at midday on August 15th, 1947, the Indian Civil Service had come to an end, and with it, after nearly nineteen years, my own service of the Crown in India. All of us, with our predecessors in the Service, over the past ninety years, since Queen Victoria's post-Mutiny proclamation of 1858, had been working towards this end, although we had not always done so consciously; and not many of us, until the last few years, had admitted that it must come in our time.

The unity of India under British rule had been such an achievement that its partition was a bitter disappointment. Yet our Indian and Pakistani colleagues were ready and able and proud to carry on the work which we had all shared together, in what were, despite partition, still two great countries.

A dividend on our work had been declared that day. Nevertheless, the stock of some of us, though far from deflated, was feeling just a trifle 'ex-div'.

'And he, that points the sentinel his room
doth license him depart at sound of morning drum.'

So I thought; but not so Lord Mountbatten. 'Don't you imagine that you are going to run away now,' he said to me. 'You are going to stay on here and help us, honorary and unpaid, for at least a fortnight. Then you can come up to Simla with us.' There was, indeed, some need for an overlap between the old and the new staff of the establishment which had just changed its name from Viceroy's House to Rashtrapati Bhavan. George Abell and the other I.C.S. officers on the old staff had been released to take up appointments outside India, and had departed: Captain Ronald Brockman R.N., now Private Secretary to the Governor General, and the new staff had hardly had time to become familiar with the normal administrative routine, which would not be greatly changed by Independence. I could provide, at any rate, a few days of continuity.

I had decided to leave government service, but to stay in India for the time being. Early in September the Mountbattens and some of their staff went up to the hills, and I went with them to join Elizabeth and our family who were already in Simla. We had been lent the Private Secretary's house in which to spend a short holiday - which, in fact, became a siege.

After a few days H.E. decided that he must return to Delhi, whence reports were reaching him that all was not well. On the evening before the Mountbattens left Simla, an ADC mentioned that they would not be seeing the Christies again as members of the staff. Should he ask them round for a drink?

'No' said Mountbatten, 'we'll go and have a drink with them'.

In the dusk we saw the Governor-General and Edwina coming across the lawn, having dismissed their ADC. It was a friendly, courteous and typical act. Before they said good-bye, H.E. produced, from some corner where he had hidden it, a parting present. It was a silver cigarette box, with an inscription engraved in his handwriting:

'In grateful memory of 145 hectic days - M of B'

7

The Taste of Freedom

The sun sets dramatically in latitude 32 North. A final burst of glory sets the distant peaks on fire, and then the colours fade swiftly, like the iridescence on dying fish, as the violet and indigo shadows move upwards from the valleys. With a shiver one realises that it is night, and a stranger far from home may well wonder how long the night will last, and what morning will bring.

It was so in the autumn of 1947 in the Simla hills. The splendour and rejoicing of the Independence Days in Delhi and Karachi had diverted attention briefly from the trouble that was brewing in Northern India. The history of the human race has shown, by many instances, that men and women of different cultures and of different religious or political persuasions can live side by side for long periods in a state, if not amity, at least apparently of neutral toleration. But when some wind fans the embers of hate and fear they are ablaze in a moment, and in the furnace the thin crust of humanity is burnt away; what is left is a savage animal.

In India, with the approach of Independence there had been a chain reaction of atrocity. Hindus, Sikhs and Moslems, living in isolated minority pockets in East Bengal, in Bihar and in the Northern Punjab had, over the previous two years, been attacked, pillaged and slaughtered with fearful savagery. These incidents provoked retaliation in other parts of India; but, although serious enough, they had been local outbursts of communal passion which either burnt themselves out or were brought under control relatively quickly.

The worst of these murderous riots happened in August 1946 and became known as the Calcutta killing. The effects were worse than elsewhere because in Calcutta the communities were more evenly matched in numbers. The Calcutta killing continued for three days, at the end of which, there were counted twenty thousand dead and wounded. It was enough, and a year later the blood-letting was not renewed, as it was in the Punjab. Bengal, after Independence, was pacified by satiety, and by the moral force of one man alone, Mahatma Gandhi – the man, not the politician – in his finest hour.

When Independence was imminent and inevitable two vast migrations began in northern India, quietly at first but increasing in volume and momentum as the days went by; two streams in opposite directions, Moslems moving westward and Hindus and Sikhs moving east.

Nothing is more helpless, pathetic and vulnerable than a stream of refugees, travelling through hostile country encumbered with children, old people and household goods, slow and determined as a line of ants. It is no part of this account to describe the terrible things that happened on that two-way exodus. The police and military commands on either side of the still undetermined frontier, including the Punjab Boundary Force of two and a half divisions under Major-General Pete Rees were not enough to provide protection over the whole of the affected area, or for migrations on the scale that were taking place. The disposition of forces had been made to control civil disturbances which were foreseen. What could not be foreseen or calculated was the ferocity of racial feeling and communalism, which would erode the loyalty of the protecting forces themselves - though with many shining examples to the contrary. It was an unlooked-for mercy that, although serious trouble was expected in the east as well as in the north-west, Bengal, having poured her sacrifice of blood a year before, and under the restraint of Gandhi's presence was now comparatively at peace, all passion spent.

In Simla there was an ominous quiet for a few days after the Mountbattens had returned to Delhi. But refugee Sikhs, many of whom had suffered or seen their brethren suffer on their way from Pakistan, were arriving daily, and when they had drawn breath they sought out innocent Moslem victims for their revenge. There was no lack of them, unsuspecting coolies, shopkeepers and domestic servants. Soon the murders began and a curfew was imposed, not only at night but for most of the day as well. I was taking a short holiday before beginning a new life and work in free India, and we were housed on what had been, until a few weeks before, the Viceregal Estate. We had charge of the Brockmans' children as well as our own, six in all. In curfew conditions the feeding of this young menagerie soon became a problem. On most days the curfew would be lifted for a few hours, and Elizabeth and I would dash out in opposite directions, to different bazaars to buy what we could find - milk and potatoes were our main objectives. We knew we should not have the advertised period of liberty, before another murder was committed and the sirens would announce that the curfew had descended again.

Elizabeth, hurrying back from the upper Mall one day, saw a Moslem hotel servant chased by Sikhs and cut down before her eyes. She rushed up to a policeman, a Hindu, who was standing in the road a few yards away and tried to drag him to the scene; but he looked the other way and passed on.

Moslem domestic servants were gathered into the protection of private houses temporarily, and some of us formed an escort after dark, defying the curfew, to conduct them by devious hill-paths to the comparative safety of the Governor-General's Estate. There we kept them under guard and fed them until they could be taken down to refugee camps in the plains, and sent on to Pakistan.

One of the volunteer escort was a Swede - what he was doing in Simla then I cannot remember - a fire-eater, who was or had been a cavalry officer. He carried a large revolver which he would sometimes brandish without provocation, and we were worried lest one night he would discharge his weapon, and draw attention to our stealthy passage.

The freshness of autumn began to change to the chill of winter, and the 'cold weather line' of dusty haze hardened over the plains below. We were cut off in Simla for a month; but gradually, with fewer unprotected Moslems left to kill, the situation was brought under control, in Simla and Delhi and in the countryside between. Arrangements could then be made for our own evacuation with a number of other families, in a road convoy under escort of the Royal Scots Fusiliers, for there were still some British troops not yet embarked from India.

The journey to Delhi, two hundred and twenty miles, was accomplished in two days, and we encamped for the night in Ambala cantonment. We passed through country where the stench or death was evidence enough of the horrors of the recent weeks.

In Delhi the situation, for a few days had been nearly out of hand. The Governor-General and his staff were a very present help to an almost desperate Nehru, not only with steadying encouragement and advice, but in a less constitutional, more practical role of helping the local officials to organise emergency measures. Many Pakistanis today must owe their lives to Edwina Mountbatten's refugee camp in the Purana Qila and to the protection arranged for them by the Governor-General of India, not without danger or without loss. Alan Campbell-Johnson and Martin Gilliat, of Mountbatten's staff, had a narrow escape when, touring the military posts at night, they failed to hear the challenge of a trigger-happy sentry. A bullet grazed Gilliat's head, and the driver of their car was killed.

For some months before Independence we had been liberally served with the slogan 'Quit India' scrawled up on walls or shouted at us in the streets. Now the British Raj had quit, but my wife and I were to stay and taste the freedom of India for more than eleven years.

Some weeks earlier I had been offered an appointment in the British Foreign Service. Several of my I.C.S. and Political Service friends had accepted posts under Her Majesty's Government: others had gone to Pakistan, and a few had remained in the service of the government of India. Elizabeth and I had pondered our own future, and decided that a change from government service would be best. Among other considerations I reckoned that I was, at forty-two, at the wrong age to be fitted comfortably into the cadre of another service. Also, we did not wish to leave India at once. We had struck some roots in Delhi, and it seemed that my nineteen years experience of working in India could best be used in India, even if outside the government service.

I had been offered another post which promised to be interesting. It was a new job of a quasi-diplomatic kind, to represent in Delhi a group of interests of which the chief constituent was Assocham - short for the Associated Chambers of Commerce and Industry in India - whose membership was predominantly, but not entirely, British. Their headquarters were in Calcutta, the commercial capital of India but at an awkward distance from the seat of government. Mountbatten and Ismay, whom I had consulted, had encouraged me to accept this offer of employment, arguing that British business interests in India, which were considerable, would need a representative in the capital to advise them in the new political context.

I accepted the offer, and became adviser in India to the Central Commercial Committee. My friend Fergus Innes, lately of the Punjab cadre of the I.C.S., became the adviser in Pakistan, and we began to fire good-tempered but highly partisan salvoes at each other across the new frontiers.

The transition to the new life was not as difficult as I imagined it might be. I had many friends, Indian and British in Delhi and Calcutta; I had easy access to most government offices in Delhi; I was allowed to continue, for a time, in occupation of my government house in York Road, as well as the office room on the now defunct European Group in the Parliament buildings, the Lok Sabha; and my new employers were patient and tolerant of my efforts to master the unfamiliar outlook and idiom of the business world.

Great friendliness from Indians immediately surrounded us. I believe that the appalling aftermath of partition had shaken their confidence and the realisation that some British people had enough faith in India's future to elect to stay in the country helped to restore it. In fact there were many who shared our faith, and the number of British in India, so far from diminishing, was to increase over the next few years.

I could not for much longer take advantage of the Government of India's hospitality by remaining in the York Road House, or in the parliamentary offices of a non-existent political party - which might also have led to misunderstanding of my function. But accommodation in Delhi for non-officials was scarce. Kind neighbours shared their house with us for a time, and, parked in their drive, the capacious motor car with which my employers had equipped me had also to serve as my office, until the local manager of Imperial Chemicals invited me and my embryo staff to occupy temporarily an unused corridor in his Connaught Circus headquarters.

The house in which we were staying was not far from Albuquerque Road, a name which was soon to be changed from that of a Portuguese viceroy to Tīs January Marg, commemorating the first black date in the calendar of independent India. In this road was the mansion and large garden of the Indian industrialist, Ganshyamdas Birla, where Mahatma Gandhi used to stay when he was in Delhi. He used also to hold his crowded prayer meetings in the garden, and it was at one of these meetings that he was assassinated on the evening on the 30th January, 1948, by a member of a fanatical Hindu sect which abhorred the doctrine of toleration which the Mahatma preached.

When I left my office on that evening I became aware, as soon as I stepped into the street, of some cause of excitement and alarm in the faces of the people, although no one in Connaught Circus knew at that stage what had happended, or could bring themselves to repeat any rumour they had heard. Sometimes in India the premonition of disaster, like the rumble of an approaching earthquake, travels faster than the news itself. At any rate, I sensed that something was amiss, and that the sooner I rejoined my family, two miles away, the better.

Ten days before, also in the grounds of Birla House, a crude bomb had exploded not far from Gandhi, This, too, may have been an attempt on his life but, probably at Gandhi's own request, there had been no noticeable tightening of security precautions. On 30th January the assassin used a pistol, and his task was easy in the throng which pressed round the Mahatma

The house where we were staying was about three hundred yards away. On that evening my wife heard what sounded like two shots from the direction of Birla House. For a few seconds after that there was dead silence, then a confused murmur of people and the noise of cars starting and moving away. It was difficult at first for those at the scene of the crime to believe what they had seen or heard, or to give a coherent account of it. For nearly an hour the truth was not generally known, and uneasy rumours were abroad. If the assassin had been a Moslem, as some were at first inclined to believe, the consequences in India, and between India and Pakistan could have been appalling. The shock, however, had stunned the people. There was no violent reaction, and the outpouring of grief and devotion at the Mahatma's funeral next day was a sufficient purging of their emotions.

Through these unsettled days our search for accommodation continued. A conversation overheard by chance at the Club caused us to make an immediate sortie to the outskirts of New Delhi, and to close a deal on the same night for a house which was unexpectedly vacant. Number Forty-seven Prithviraj Road was to be our home for the remaining five years of our time in Delhi. It stood opposite the tomb of Safdar Jung, commander of Mogul armies, a delicately ornate building of red sandstone and white marble, surmounted by an onion-shaped dome which glowed red at night as a warning to aircraft approaching Willingdon Airport. My office was also moved, to a warren-like group of wartime hutments, which had once housed the nerve-centre of the U.S. Army's comunications system. Accommodation of any kind in Delhi in those days had to be schemed, intrigued and fought for. It was said that some newly-arrived foreign diplomatic Missions, occupying hotel suites, were glad enough to find a spare bathroom in which to set up their Chanceries.

Our life now settled down to an easier routine. It was a routine with a difference, for the social and political atmosphere in New Delhi was changing, more noticeably than in the surrounding countryside, though perhaps not so obviously as in the smaller towns of Northern India.

The change in social atmosphere was the more apparent at first, and for this three things were mainly responsible: the emergence of Indian women, the influx of refugees, mostly Sikhs, and the arrival of the Corps Diplomatique.

Although we had many Indian men friends, it had not always been easy, before independence, to meet and get to know their wives and daughters, as persons rather than decorative adjuncts to social functions and ceremony. Their men-folk, whether government servants or professional men, were as a rule quite at ease in western society. Many had travelled outside India and had adopted western manners and conventions. They would dine out, take part in games, and in all that the Club provided, with apparent satisfaction, but not many would bring their wives with them. This may have been due to shyness on the part of the women, to a distaste for unfamiliar customs or to a stronger nationalist prejudice than their menfolk felt - for women, I have noticed, are often capable of more extreme political feeling and expression than men. Some survival of the restrictions of purdah may also have been responsible.

Some early signs of social change after independence appeared in that stronghold of western imperial manners, the New Delhi Gymkhana Club. It had always been a 'mixed' club, and its membership was a status symbol that survived and, surprisingly, was enhanced by independence. In fact, the Committee of the Club, now predominantly Indian, were far more strict about the admission of any whom they supposed to be parvenu 'counter-jumpers' or of immigrant Sikhs than their British predecessors would have been. The few Sikhs who were admitted certainly caused some problems. A notice appeared by the swimming pool, 'Gentlemen with long hair are requested to wear bathing caps' - for the long hair was also liberally oiled.

But the Gymkhana Club provided the first evidence of the emergence of Indian women, not only of the westernised minority of them, into 'society'. At the Club dances, groups would at first gather round the room, bunches of gay wallflowers, not venturing onto the floor, but observing the dancers with keen and wistful curiosity. It was not long before the younger ones could be persuaded to join in the scandalous gyrations. Then the ice was broken, and Indian women began to take their rightful place as hostesses and leaders of society in their own capital city, contributing by their appearance, their wit and gaiety to the pleasure of life, whereby we were all immeasurably benefited.

Another change was caused by the arrival of numerous embassies, high commissions and smaller diplomatic missions in the capital. Such was the pressure of accommodation that some of them had to make do, at first, with quarters far beneath their dignity - like the bathroom Chanceries already mentioned. This shortage of housing for distinguished new arrivals soon caused the disappearance of my favourite riding ground, which I had thought to be safe, for historical reasons - the open country between the Delhi Ridge and the Qutb Minar, extending from the Commander-in-Chief's house, now appropriated by Pandit Nehru as Prime Minister, to Palam airport - a plain scattered over with the ruined tombs and palaces and highways of forgotten dynasties. The bulldozers moved in to prepare it for the construction of a 'diplomatic enclave' - some called it a ghetto - and five years later it had taken on the appearance of an international exhibition site, crowded with a nightmarish medley of architectural styles. New Delhi soon became a cosmopolitan city. Our children went to international schools and happily mixed with every variety of race and language. The noise of the Tower of Babel could not have equalled the polyglot riot of sound on their playgrounds. One of our son Robin's

school-fellows was 'Tiger' Pataudi, and the shock of
recognition, at a later date, on more famous playing fields, may
have had something to do with the early fall of the young
Nawab's wicket, fine batsman though he was, when Robin came on
to bowl.

The sedateness of British manners left Delhi unprepared for
the impact with those of other nationals, and this sometimes led
to diplomatic contretemps. A French military attaché, who used
to wear a flower through a bullet hole in the lobe of his ear -
acquired, he said, during the 'resistance' - carelessly backed
his car into another standing in front of the Club. The owner
of the injured car, an Indian lady, proceeded to give him a
piece of her mind in English. He walked away remarking, rudely
but distinctly, 'Va-t-en, vache!' But the lady had lived in
Paris, and could understand honest French; and, although a
Hindu, she was not mollified by the ingenious explanation that
the Frenchman, believing Hindus held cows in reverence, was
trying to pay her a compliment. The scandal caused the
attaché's embassy hurriedly to discover that he was already
under orders of transfer.

On another occasion a Latin-American diplomat, who insisted
on whistling and cracking nuts during a cabaret show had a
flower vase emptied over his head by an airline pilot, who
happened to be a friend of the artiste. Legal action ensued,
but when the foreigner claimed diplomatic privilege to excuse
him from attending court, the Indian magistrate would have none
of it, and summarily dismissed his complaint.

I have often wondered how much of the mischief that women
can do, quite innocently of course, in diplomatic circles is
officially reported. I witnessed two incidents which could have
caused enough loss of face, if not scandal, to set the
international wires humming.

The Soviet ambassador was saying good-night to his hostess,
the wife of another ambassador, in front of the assembled
guests. He seized her hand in a bear-like grip, whereat she let
out a loud wail. He backed away in confusion while she slowly
drew four rings off her fingers. 'Now, Mr. Ambassador, she
said, 'you may shake hands with me.'

Another time, about Christmas, guests were taking leave of
the wife of a senior diplomat. The head of the Mission stood in
front of her, and she lifted her face to be kissed. He was the
picture of embarrassment. He looked round wildly; he looked up
and saw a bunch of mistletoe. 'Oh-ah-yes, I see, mistletoe,' he
said. 'But do we need an excuse?' she asked sweetly.

We saw a good deal of successive British High Commissioners
and of their staff in those days. Sir Terence Shone, the first,
had been en poste for some months before Independence, with Alec

Symon, his Deputy, and Roland Owen, the Senior Trade Commissioner. The pace of events had taken them rather by surprise, and immense responsibilities, as representatives of the Crown and of British nationals in India, had suddenly descended on their shoulders, before they were adequately staffed. Alec Symon, to whom I had to report my decision not to accept the offer of a Foreign Service post in Pakistan, assured me that, even if I had accepted it, he would not have let me leave Delhi. I am not sure that I should have relished such high-jacking at the outset of a new career.

Britain was admirably represented in India during those early years of Independence. Shone's successor was Sir Archibald Nye, who had been Deputy Chief of the Imperial General Staff, and Governor of Madras immediately before the transfer of power. After him came Sir Alexander Clutterbuck, whose father had been Inspector-General of Forests in India, and left his memorial in the exotically named town of Clutterbuckgunje; and, after we had left Delhi, Malcolm MacDonald, a man whose intelligence was as keen as his sympathies were wide, and who had to wrestle, among other problems, with the uncongenial task of explaining the Suez venture to audiences almost as incredulous as he was himself. Pandit Nehru, I was told, received the news early in the morning while standing on his head in the middle of a yogic exercise. It would be nice to think that Malcolm MacDonald, who also practised yoga, had to adopt the same posture in order to deliver it.

These High Commissioners were ably supported by a succession of Deputies who were themselves destined for distinguished service, including Frank Roberts and Joe (Saville) Garner.

This was a period when the non-official British in India were having to accustom themselves, not always easily, to the realities of a change of government; to understand that the British High Commissioner was in India to represent not their interests directly, but those of his Government; to recognise that the consular functions of the High Commissioner did not amount to a protective shield, and that it behove them to organise themselves to watch their own interests and to establish proper relations directly with the Government of India. Some adjustments along these lines were also having to take place among the officers of the High Commission.

My own function, as representative in Delhi of British industrial and trading interests, as well as of the United Kingdom Citizens Association, kept me very much in touch with this process of adjustment, and enabled me in some measure to assist it. I was greatly helped, in turn, by the friendliness and trust of many Indians who had been my colleagues, and by the invariable kindness of successive British High Commissioners and their staff. As the number of the latter in Delhi increased rapidly without having a place to lay their heads, we were privileged to have several High Commission officers staying with us at various times in Prithviraj Road.

The other post-Independence changes of atmosphere in Delhi were of a political kind, and it did not need particularly sensitive antennae to pick them up. There were no strong manifestations of racial or of nationalist feeling – in the pre-partition sense – for the aftermath of Independence was warm with friendship and gratitude to the British; and in remoter parts of the surrounding countryside one met with incredulity and openly expressed regret at their departure. There were, however, strong undercurrents in the domestic politics of the sub-continent, and the massacre of refugees on both sides of the border had left relations between India and Pakistan an open wound which would not be easily healed. The wound was kept open by bitter disputes over refugee property and by border 'incidents'; and especially by the unresolved questions of the accession of three Princes' States – Junagadh, Kashmir and Hyderabad – in each of which the ruler's religion was different from that of the majority of his people.

The story of that bitterness has been told and debated at length, and is not yet ended. This is not the place to recount it; but it might have been otherwise if I had accepted a suggestion from Philip Mason (alias Woodruff), with whom I had sailed for India twenty years earlier. He already had to his credit some of the best novels that have been written about India, and later he was to be the historian of the men who had ruled it. He was now tutoring the grandsons of His Exalted Highness the Nizam of Hyderabad, and asked me if I would consider taking over the duties from him. Had we been in Hyderabad in September, 1948, when the Indian army marched in, there might have been a tale to tell.

Or if we had been holidaying in Kashmir when, at the end of October 1947, well-supported 'tribesmen' from Pakistan invaded the Kashmir valley, and Indian troops were air-lifted to meet and repel them in the outskirts of Srinagar. We had just returned to Delhi from being besieged in Simla and, from our house near the Willingdon airport we could hear the commandeered aircraft of all descriptions taking off throughout the night on an operation, which, for successful improvisation, deserves to be, perhaps is, a model for study in military Staff Colleges.

The strongest undercurrent in Indian domestic politics was

the rivalry between Pandit Jawaharlal Nehru and Sardar Vallabhbhai Patel. The two strong men of the Congress Party were utterly different in character and outlook – Nehru, the younger, Western educated, a socialist intellectual; Patel, a hard-boiled veteran, a Gujerati than which there is no more home-spun Indian, a Congress Tory of the deepest blue.

Gandhi had been aware of the mutual antipathy of these two, and of the danger in it for India; and, in the last days of his life, he had tried to bring about a reconciliation, or at any rate to exact a promise of co-operation. In this he must have succeeded to some extent, for the incompatibility never became an open breach, and Patel's death in 1950 resolved their difference.

It was in a New Delhi theatre at that time that we saw a reflection of the public awareness of this private rift. The occasion was a performance by a touring company from England of scenes from Shakespeare. Many educated Indians combine an inborn political consciousness with a keen induced appreciation of Shakespeare. They have benefited, unlike most British children by being brought up on Shakespeare from a tender age, and from having learned long passages of his plays by heart.
The theatre was packed, and members of the audience were throughly enjoying themselves, repeating aloud the familiar speeches in a continuous low murmur simultaneously with the actors, sometimes even ahead of them.
Inevitably the programme included extracts from 'Julius Caesar', and the quarrel scene between Brutus and Cassius. Immediately the audience caught the echo of current politics. They craned their necks to see whether the protagonists were in the theatre to enjoy the analogy; and they asked each other audibly 'Where is Jawaharlal? Is Sardarji here?'
Shakespeare would have been delighted by their intelligent appreciation of a political reference which, possibly, he too had intended to be applied to a pair of his own contemporaries.
Patel had set himself a task which he was probably better equipped to do than Nehru, the integration of the Princes' States with the rest of India. The days of the velvet glove, patient negotiation and respect for treaties made with the Raj were over. This needed a strong and ruthless hand, and it was applied. Patel's main instrument for this was V.P. Menon, a man after his own heart who, starting as a clerk in a government office, had become a fine constitutional lawyer. He had advised Mountbatten and his predecessors in the negotiations leading to Independence, and I had worked with him closely myself.
His treatment was drastic, but there is little doubt that

India's body politic was the healthier for it. The best of the Princes and their States were preserved in the new territorial divisions; the rest were compensated, more or less, and merged with oblivion.

Ironically, much the same fate eventually overtook V.P.Menon - and it is worth a digression to record it. He was an unusual man, being an Indian patriot who had a genuine admiration of the British and their institutions. Two powerful sponsors had assisted his own exceptional talents in his rise to the influential position which he came to occupy, first the government of British India which had recognised his worth and had received his loyal service; then Sardar Vallabhbhai Patel, who became his patron after Independence. When these two supports were removed in quick succession Menon was left exposed to the envy of lesser men and the malice of those in high places whom he had not troubled to court. He disappeared prematurely from public life, but made good use of his retirement by writing two masterly books on the transfer of power in India and the integration of the States, which are likely to remain the leading historical text books of the period.

It cannot be denied that national independence, at whatever cost achieved and whatever problems it brings in its train, brings also, in its early days, an exhilaration and a zest to all who breathe its air. Those were happy and stimulating days in Delhi. Our son David flew out to us for the school holidays, and the whole family were, for the first time, united. David's visit was short, but long enough for him to give mumps to the rest of the family, from which they spent the summer recuperating in Kasauli. This is a small hill station below Simla, and near enough to Delhi for me to be able to join the invalids for occasional week-ends.

Our house was full of a succession of varied and delightful guests and lodgers. As well as homeless members of the British High Commission, there came research scholars, travelling ecclesiastics, military advisers and journalists, and many other interesting people. Hotels in Delhi might be full, but there was usually room at Forty-seven Prithviraj Road, even if some of the visitors had to sleep out in rows on the back lawn. If it was high summer, when for weeks on end the thermometer did not fall below 90 at night, the sleepers on the lawn were provided with buckets of water by their beds, instead of fans, so that they could sprinkle their scorching mattresses from time to time for the brief respite of coolth by evaporation, until, with first light the morning flight of screaming green parrots would finally end their troubled slumbers and drive them indoors.

Among our soldier guests were Brigadier Akehurst and his

wife. 'Beau' Akehurst was a Canadian who had falsified his age
during World War I in order to join the British army, but had
spent most of his life with the Indian army as a signals
specialist, in which capacity he had chosen to remain with them
after Independence. Another who stayed with us was Adrienne
Farrell, who must be one of the most conscientious and able
journalists who have ever served a news agency. She was
genuinely distressed when a cable arrived from her principals in
London to the effect: 'You scooped by such-and-such agency
Bihar famine. 'How?' There was no famine in Bihar, but the
peremptory 'How?' was tantamount to an order to go and find and
report on one. Miss Farrell knew well enough that press reports
which mentioned famine or its possibility, when there was
nothing more serious than a manageable shortage, could
precipitate disaster. She reported the truth honestly, but got
little thanks for it.

I was helped in my own work by a small competent Indian
staff, and by Mrs. Betty Kitcat, an invaluable aide who, after a
distinguished wartime service with the Red Cross had also
decided to stay in India.
My duties were two-way representation. I had to interpret
the policies of the Government of India to my employers in
Calcutta and elsewhere, and to represent the view of the
business community to Delhi. There were also a number of
All-India Councils and Committees formed for various purposes at
the centre of Government, and I would find myself nominated as
the Associated Chambers' representative on these. I attended a
meeting of one such committee in the Prime Minister's house,
when G.D. Birla, the financier-industrialist, was the only other
person present who was not clothed in snowy homespun; in fact,
all the rest were members of the Congress Working Committee,
the most powerful political body in India. There was nothing
political on our agendas, of course, or I should not have been
there: our purpose was to raise money for a memorial to Sardar
Patel. There was nearly an undignified scuffle before this
meeting began. As I saw other members removing their shoes and
preparing to sit cross-legged on the floor, I did likewise; but
Jagjivan Ram, (then Labour Minister) tried to prevent me.
'You cannot do that. It is not your custom, though it is
ours. Please sit in a chair.'
'Look here, sir, 'I protested, 'how would you like it if
you went to London, and they insisted that you should sit on the
floor, while they sat in chairs, because it is your custom?'
Even Nehru, who was sparing with his laughter, smiled.
In fact, Nehru had a quiet sense of humour, although it was
not often in evidence. He could sometimes unbend, and I had

first hand experience of one of the rare occasions.

For many years past it had been the practice that, when two or three Etonians could be gathered together on the Fourth of June in Delhi or Simla, they would dine together, with the Viceroy as host if he also happened to be an Etonian. If he were not, some message of greeting and condolence in dog Latin would be composed and sent to him. On this particular schoolboy festival in 1948 it happened that Lord Mountbatten was himself giving a private dinner to Nehru and Rajagopalachari, the South Indian veteran statesman who was to succeed Mountbatten as Governor-General. The assembled Old Etonians duly composed and sent their message, not expecting any acknowledgement or reply; but back it came, in Nehru's hand and best Urdu - better than his spoken Hindi - beginning: 'Purane Eton ke vidyalarthi....' the whole of which being translated read: 'To the Old Boys of Eton who are enjoying themselves in Delhi to-day, we, who have had the opportunity and proud privilege of being educated at Dartmouth, Madras and Harrow send greetings on this occasion to our brothers who had no such luck, and only went to Eton.' I managed to purloin and keep the original.

At another Eton dinner, post-Independence, two of our scant number were the brothers Kumaramangalam, one a soldier and later to be Chief of Army Staff - equivalent to Commander-in-Chief - and the other a civil servant. They had another Etonian brother, and a sister, both politically active communists who - communists being unpopular in India at that time - were temporarily incommunicado. They told me a story about the communist brother. When he had been at Cambridge he had stood for election as President of the Union, and succeeded. He stood again another year, but failed. He explained it thus: 'The first time I had plenty of support; the Indian, the communist and the Etonian votes were solid for me. Next time, unfortunately, the left wing and the Indian votes were split: only the Etonians were loyal.'

There was a revival of polo in New Delhi. Polo had been here before the war, but in those days when crack cavalry regiments, British and Indian, were still stationed in Delhi cantonments, it had been polo of a high standard. The new polo club provided only 'station polo', and the beginners who took the field in slow chukkers outnumbered those who had some experience of the game. The young Indian officers of the Governor-General's Bodyguard were keen, but beginners too. They provided a ground and maintained it, and paraded their sowars or troopers to blow the bugle and collect the balls. The club bought and trained ponies which could be hired, for few members had more than one pony of their own.

Polo in New Delhi, 1951: (The three riders on left of group are Nawab of Pataudi, Rao Raja Hanut Singh and John Christie)

We were an extraordinary mixture: generals and air marshals, soldiers and sailors, civilians, diplomats, businessmen, princes - and one courageous girl - Sheila Stevenson, step-daughter of Sir Archibald Nye, the British High Commissioner. She was a competent player, and if one forbore, out of chivalry, from swearing at her or riding her off too roughly, she soon made it clear that she was not prepared to reciprocate. Perhaps the most remarkable player was a naval attaché of the American Embassy. He had been a submarine commander, and a victim of polio not long before he was posted to a shore job in Delhi. He had been advised to exercise all his muscles, for which purpose swimming and riding are the best activities; and he had barely learned to ride when he became an addicted polo player. So enthusiastically did he practise to improve his game that within two years he had become one of the best players of our club, awarded a goal handicap that made no allowance for his physical infirmity.

The existence of the Delhi Polo Club soon attracted the attention of some of our princely neighbours who were world-famous polo players, practically lived for the game and could resist no opportunity of playing it. The Maharajah of Jaipur arranged to keep a string of ponies in Delhi and would fly over from his palace, one hundred and fifty miles away, with some of his staff, to join in our mid-week game. Rao Raja Hanut Singh used to came often from Jodhpur, sometimes carrying a bagful of trophies, and would organise an impromptu tournament to play for them. One of these matches was the sad occasion of the death of the Nawab of Pataudi, famous cricketer and father of Robin's friend 'Tiger'. Like Jaipur, twenty years later, he died on the field, apparently from a heart attack, in the middle of a game. Pataudi was a great loss: he was an exceptional person, not only as an all-round athlete, but - a portent in those days - a Moslem prince in the Indian Foreign Service.

Those international polo players who joined in our slow and 'twelve anna' chukkers, did so without the slightest condescension; and with their example and encouragement the standard of our play improved rapidly. New Delhi attracted visiting teams, from the Argentine and elsewhere, and the Polo Club was soon organising its own high-class tournaments. I had not played polo myself for fifteen years, but I picked up the game again and enjoyed myself enormously, playing and umpiring.

I wear spectacles, but not for polo. The fact that I did not keep to this rule on horseback at other times nearly ended my equestrian career, for I had two falls, once out hunting - the Delhi pack commuted between Meerut, across the river, and the capital - and once on an ordinary, lazy morning hack ; too lazy, in fact, because I let my mare put her foot in a hole. On both occasions my glasses broke and I cut my face badly, and was lucky not to lose an eye.

The visiting President of the Associated Chambers was therefore suitably impressed when he found his representative in Delhi swathed in bandages and regarding him balefully out of one eye.

The President of 'Assocham' changed every year, so that I had the privilege of serving under a succession of eminent businessmen. They were, in those days, the heads of the leading Managing Agency companies in India, those peculiarly British-Indian institutions which were the commercial successors of the East India Company. Managing Agencies provided the finance, management and other services, the protective shade under which the tender growth of new companies and budding industries could develop to their full potential. This was and is still true of the best managing agencies; later imitators distorted and depreciated them for less admirable ends.

I had often to visit Calcutta, and sometimes other parts of India as well. On one such official expedition I penetrated to the deep south, where subscribers to the Central Committee's fund felt out of touch with events. When I reached Munnaar, in the High Range of Travancore, I was not surprised that they found themselves isolated. Here, in the cool highlands of tea plantations and smooth-turfed downs, it was still regarded by some of the residents as a 'white man's country', four years after Independence. The planters grew and processed tea, played rugby and fished trout streams in their spare time, remote and blissfuly unaware of, and largely uninterested in what was happening outside their mountain fastness.

A few days before I arrived, an unfamiliar phenomenon had disturbed the leaders of the British community in Munnaar. A jeep had invaded their sanctuary from the plains below, flying a sinister red flag emblazoned with the hammer and sickle. The Indian occupants proceeded, without permission, to hold a meeting in the middle of the tea planters' township, and made what sounded to their astonished ears some highly seditious speeches.

'What is our Association going to do about it?' they asked me, 'What is the British High Commission doing?'

It had not occured to them to discuss the incident with the Indian local officials, and they seldom had any need to visit Trivandrum, the headquarters of the State government down in the plains. Patient explanation was necessary of the changes which the transfer of power had brought about in their lives, and in the relative responsibilities of governments, their representatives and their foreign guests.

After five years as Adviser in New Delhi I felt it was time for a change. No representative should represent for too long. However carefully he treads, he cannot, if he does his job properly, always avoid treading in tender places; and if he treads on any exalted corns, he is not thereafter likely to be so useful to those whom he represents. So far, I believe, I had avoided any serious <u>faux</u> <u>pas</u>. I had built up the office of the Adviser, made and fostered the right contacts; and now an assistant had joined me who was fully competent to take over and carry on my work.

My employers therefore agreed to release me, to join a post which I had been offered with the British India Corporation of Kanpur, an industrial city of Uttar Pradesh - more recognisable, perhaps, as Cawnpore in the United Provinces. I believed it would be interesting to learn some more about business from the business end. In this I was not to be disappointed.

In November 1952 we said good-bye to New Delhi, which had been our home for fifteen years; but we were sure we had not seen the last of it. It was still dark when we crossed the Jumna, and the sun was rising through the mist over the Ganges at Garmukhtesar. Then we drove north-east towards the Himalayas, bound for a holiday in Ranikhet, the small hill station where my mother had been born, north of Naini Tal.

Ranikhet was now a ghost station, a deserted cantonment, empty boarding houses; but there was a magnificent view across the Garhwal hills to the high peaks of the Himalayas. Ten of them were in sight, from Nalikanta to Nanda Kot, all over 20,000 feet, with Kamet away to the west and Nanda Devi right in front of us, both towering three or four thousand feet above the rest. It was a great refreshment just to watch for a few days the changing shadows and colours of the snows, in the clear, sharp air of early winter.

Then we turned our faces south, passed through Lucknow and crossed the Ganges again into Kanpur.

8
The Business End

The form, the substance and the shadows of national independence vary according to the angle of vision of the beholder. An aboriginal in the Orissa hills could point to an aeroplane overhead and claim that it was Mahatma Gandhi, who had sprouted wings like the Garuda bird, flying back from victories over the British Raj; the Indian politician or administrator, with a shudder of apprehension, prepared to pick up the white man's burden which his recent masters, with familiar eccentricity but only half-expected generosity, had recently deposited at his feet; the old cook of the officers' mess in Ranikhet who came, wrapped in a blanket, to gossip with us on a verandah facing the Himalayan snows, was not yet resigned five years after the event, to the cruel blow of fate which had changed his life. We bought his excellent fudge and chutney, and encouraged him to revive the memories of past prestige and happiness with talk of long-departed men and regiments. In return he presented us reverently with a very early edition of Mrs. Beeton's Cookery Book. It was the laying up of his colours.

The five years which we had spent in New Delhi since Independence Day had provided rewarding experiences, but it had not always been easy to realise that one was living in India, and not, say, in a sub-tropical Cheltenham. After the bloody early weeks of the refugee migrations and the assassination of Gandhi, when passions had subsided and the stunned bewilderment had passed, the capital seemed to assume a cloak of self-conscious dignity, and to affect an almost British understatement of its problems and anxieties. Having a new status as well as an old tradition to maintain, Delhi did not welcome the condescensions of well-meaning foreigners like Mr. Chester Bowles, the American ambassador. He tried to demonstrate his republican sympathy for an under-developed country by moving out of his palatial residence to a humbler dwelling, and exchanging his Cadillac for a bicycle; but he was regarded by Indians as an eccentric for his pains. The inherited prestige of the imperial past was hard to exorcise; one felt that the power was still as it had been for centuries 'the power that stands on privilege, and goes with women and champagne and bridge' or their equivalents. Not so much champagne, perhaps; gone were the days when a British Governor could send to an Indian political prisoner in goal - Motilal Nehru, Jawaharlal's father - a case of what he knew to be his favourite vintage, because they had been old friends; and respect was due, in the capital of India, to the ruling party's ideological prejudice against alchohol, which had been enshrined in the new Constitution. But the enforcement of this in Delhi was not onerous; one token 'dry day' a week, when the liquor shops were closed and one could not buy a hard drink in a restaurant. In the hotels, considerate room bearers would warn guests on the day before to stock up with their requirements of whisky; and in private houses there was no restriction, except that of the purse. The cost of living had risen to £5 a bottle, except for duty-free members of the diplomatic corps; and for some reason the superior brands were usually only to be found in Indian households.

But New Delhi was not Indian India. That was to be found in Uttar Pradesh, the northern province, the northern limits, almost, of John Company's rule, in the heart of Aryavarta, whither we were now bound.

'India, that is Bharat, that is Uttar Pradesh' was an ironical parody of the preamble to the Constitution, quoted, no doubt enviously by an Indian outsider, a Prime Minister of Bengal, but certainly accepted as nothing but the truth in the U.P. Here, in Oudh, and the land of the Two Rivers, of the great cities of Lucknow, Kanpur, Benares and Allahabad, we were to experience during the next six years the realities of a transfer of power, not political only but economic and industrial as well.

An insignificant riverside village in 1800, Kanpur gave its name to a large military cantonment, from which developed the untidy industrial city of today. Two years of its history were soaked in blood, for it was the hinge of the Indian Mutiny campaign of 1857-58. The cantonment on the south bank of the Ganges was originally an encampment of the East India Company's troops, sent under the terms of the Company's treaty with the Nawab Wazir of Oudh to protect his lands from his enemies. Fifty years later the cynical policy of those days found excuses for this army to cross the river and annex the territory. A main cause of the Sepoy Revolt was not greased cartridges so much as the resentment in Upper India which this and other annexations aroused.

Meanwhile the army needed tents and clothing, boots,

harness, saddlery and munitions. Factories sprang up to supply them, and these were still the main industries of Kanpur at the end of 1952.

It is an unlovely city, relieved, in and around, by occasional oases of greenness, quiet and beauty. The judder of looms and the stench of tanneries, when the wind was in the wrong direction, became part of our daily life, and we soon ceased to notice them; but, after Delhi, we found Kanpur lacking in architectural distinction. Its best aspect is from the river, the south bank of which is lined with temples and the steps of bathing ghats, giving it the appearance of a smaller Benares.

The driving force of most religions is the quest for salvation and the remission of sins. It was impressive to see the stream of devout humanity drawn daily in their thousands to the riverside by the purifying power, in life and death, of Ganges water; and sad to observe how many priests and beggars there were to profit by this devotion, and fleece the faithful on their way.

The British India Corporation Limited, which I had been invited to join as deputy managing director, was the largest industrial group in Upper India and included cotton and woollen textile mills, the North-West Tanneries and Cooper Allens, which was the biggest manufacturer in India of army boots, harness and other leather goods. The B.I.C. had recently also taken over Begg Sutherlands, a managing agency company which embraced more textile mills - of which the best known was Elgin Mills, famous throughout Asia for tents and towels - a number of sugar factories and a variety of smaller concerns.

Sir Alexander MacRobert had founded the Corporation thirty years before I joined it, by combining several existing concerns, and, after a shaky start, it had prospered. After his death there had been troubles on the Board from which Robert Menzies, a Scottish accountant, had emerged, with the support of Sir Alexander's strong-minded American widow, as chairman and managing director.

A charitable trust had been set up as a memorial to Sir Alexander and to his four sons, all killed in the war or in flying accidents; and among the investments of this trust was a controlling interest in the B.I.C. It proved to be the Corporation's Achilles heel.

The B.I.C's contribution to India's war effort had been considerable. It had thrived on valuable government contracts, but after the war the machinery of its factories and the energies of its top management were both rather the worse for wear.

There was a historical fascination about Kanpur, apart from its grim Mutiny associations. It was a dynastic city, truly Indian, but with a strong flavouring of generations of British families whose enterprise had built it. Alongside the British dynasties had grown and prospered the Indian commercial families whose forebears, originally moneylenders and bankers, had helped to finance the enterprise, had graduated in the next generation to be agents and partners, and finally had become owners of the industries themselves; for many of the British family interests had been sold out to Indians after the war, and with the approach of Independence. The B.I.C. was left, at the time that I joined it, as the largest and almost the last of the British-controlled and managed companies.

Sir Robert Menzies was the uncrowned king of Kanpur, but some of the Indian industrialists could have rivalled him if they had not been perpetually quarrelling and litigating among themselves, the Singhanias, Jaipurias, Srivastavas, Baglas and the rest. The intrigues in Kanpur were worthy of medieval Florence.

This comparatively long tradition of Indo-British association in Kanpur was brought home to me by a conversation with Pandit Govind Ballabh Pant, an elderly freedom-fighter without a trace of rancour, who was then Chief Minister of Uttar Pradesh.

'How is your Club getting on?' he asked me one day when I had come over from Kanpur to Lucknow to see him on some business. 'I suppose Prohibition makes some difficulties for you; but you must have got a licence to supply permit-holders?'.

Kanpur, being an industrial area, was subject to prohibition laws more strictly enforced than in Delhi. No hard liquor was sold in the Club bar, in order to avoid discrimination, because Indian members (although usually well supplied at home) could not easily get permits to buy the stuff legally. Europeans had only to declare themselves addicts in order to obtain permits, and took care to be well-heeled with hip flasks when they visited the Club, out of which they could invite their Indian friends to sample their 'barley sherbet'.

There was no point in explaining all this to Pandit Pant: he was probably well aware of it already.

'No, sir' I said, 'we have not applied for a club permit. Most of our members are Indian, you know.'

'Ah, yes: a pity you don't exclude Indians. You would have no problem then.' There was a twinkle in his eye.

'You are joking, Panditji. Why should we exclude Indians? We have always been a mixed club in Kanpur, and are proud of our racial mixture. We would not think of excluding Welshmen or

Yorkshiremen; and you should see our Indian members dancing a reel on St. Andrew's night.'

He laughed. 'You are right; I was not serious. And I agree that it is a good thing to hold on to the best of old associations, where one can. You know, I believe you British must have been quite human when you smoked huqqas, and had Indian wives and mistresses.'

Race consciousness and the practice of segregation are nothing new in India's social history, and their outward and visible signs, the customs of purdah and the taboos of caste and untouchability, have as little commendable about them as South African apartheid. But between European and Indian there had been surprisingly little manifestation of a colour bar before easier travel brought out more white women, the evangelical movement imported religious intolerance, and the Mutiny and its suppression left bitter memories which could not be effaced in a generation or two. Many ghosts of the Mutiny walked in Kanpur and Lucknow, and we were conscious of them while we lived there, nearly a hundred years after the events; but they were not so substantial as to obscure an occasional flash-back to the less constrained relationships of the eighteenth century.

Such thoughts gave no solace to Robert Menzies, the chairman and managing director of the British Indian Corporation. He was tired of India and longed for home. It was now his practice to spend six months of every year in England, and he intended to retire completely after two or three years. Sir Arthur Inskip, his deputy for many years, had recently died. It was with an eye to the succession (and I hope not with an eye to my comparative innocence in business matters) that Menzies had invited me to join the B.I.C.

I had a lot to learn, and some of the first things I learned were that the reins of management had fallen slack; that the B.I.C. had been living on its fat, and that hidden reserves were being used to maintain high dividends, which should have been used to replace worn out plant. For years no one had stood up to Robert Menzies on the Board, but this nettle had to be grasped.

I had an invaluable mentor and support in Ronald Powell, a young man of great energy and ability from the Begg Sutherland side of the business, who had been brought on to the B.I.C. Board at the same time as myself. We had also the support of another director, Rai Bahadur Ram Narain, an elderly banker, whose knowledge of Kanpur's turbulent history and whose fund of highly-spiced anecdote about its former buccaneer captains of industry were unrivalled. It was wise counsel as well as entertainment to hear his cautionary tales delivered in a fine classical style of the age of English elegance. Together we three managed to persuade the Board that the dividend must be reduced, in keeping with the real state of affairs. But Menzies never forgave us, and this decision had repercussions later.

Meanwhile there was plenty to be done, to find the means of restoring the B.I.C. to health, to learn my business and to get to know my new surroundings and the outposts of the B.I.C. empire.

We had a fine mansion of a house, not far from the river but without a view of it. It had a wide sweep of lawn, avenues of majestic blue gum trees and innumerable flowering shrubs. Our gardeners plied a profitable trade by selling the flowers to the Hindu faithful as they flocked to the river bank to make their offerings; but there were enough for all.

The soil of the Doab, between the Ganges and the Jumna is fertile, and our garden gave ample scope for my wife's expertise; but the gardeners were horrified if they saw either Elizabeth or myself surreptitiously taking spade or trowel in our hands. Not only did it seem to cause them acute embarrassment and discomfort, there was a touch of trade unionism and restrictive practice about it as well. Inside the house, too, there were some servants who would only dust above the level of their elbows; stooping was for inferiors, and as for going down on hands and knees, that was for sweepers, a different caste of servant altogether. Domestic service has always been a labour-intensive occupation in India, and in an over-populated country it is understandable that to step outside the limits of one's job is to deprive another of livelihood, not simply to lose caste - for Moslem servants were almost as particular as Hindus in this respect. It was a phenomenon peculiar to the households of Europeans and rich Indians, and the coming of Independence made no difference to it. We were compelled by social customs not ours, to employ far more servants than we needed.

Our servants' quarters in Kanpur housed the population of a small village community, and the inhabitants were certainly not always our own servants and their families. We had a kind of feudal responsibility for their health and welfare; even for their debts and their law-suits, their domestic quarrels and encounters with the police required from time to time our seigneurial intervention. Students of comparative religion or of communal co-existence would have found these quarters a fruitful field for research, for we had among our servants not only Hindus and Moslems, but Christians and Buddhists, and even - a legacy from our predecessor - a Sikh, who had some pretension to the priesthood, for he had converted, without permission, a spare room into a small gurdwara and installed in it the Holy Granth Sahib, the Sikh bible which is diplayed in temples as an object of worship. This conferred an odour of sanctity on our back yard, but also attracted quite a congregation of the guru's co-religionists. Lest the place of worship should become a permanency and create an awkward precedent - we had visions of an outcrop of mosques, temples and other shrines - we had to ask him to remove his scriptures and himself elsewhere.

The demands of the B.I.C. office, and of a household far larger than we had ever controlled, before or since, could have tied us to headquarters if we had not determined to escape them sometimes, with a clear conscience, by going on tour. An advantage of Indian 'up country' domestic arrangements is that one can walk out of the house at five minutes notice, for an absence of a week, a month, a year, and return to find everything (more or less) in order, and carry on as if there had been no interruption.

Our first visits were to sugar factories managed by Begg Sutherlands, some in north Bihar and some in the Terai, the submontane plain on the border of Nepal, from which in winter one could see a line of Himalayan snow peaks floating above the dust haze.

Sugar cane in northern India is grown in small-holdings which are 'tied' to factories, and not in large plantations as in most other sugar-growing parts of the world. One result of this is that, in a year when cane is in short supply because of floods or other accidents, there is much surreptitious poaching on neighbours' preserves, and even pitched battles between the retainers of adjoining estates are not unknown. The quality of the cane is not of the best in this part of India. The soil and climate are far from ideal for sugar-cane, which was hurriedly introduced, in the latter part of the nineteenth century, as a substitute cash crop for indigo, when aniline dyes had ruined that industry. Also, the local government fixes the price of cane (with the democratic object of catching the growers' votes) not by quality, that is by juice content, but by weight. The grower, therefore, has no incentive to improve the quality of his cane, but loads his bullock cart with stalks as thick as old bamboos, all fibre and very little juice; he often throws in a brick of two for good measure, to cheat the factory weigh-bridges.

Some of the mills were built on the sites of old indigo factories, which once flourished in Bihar and Bengal. One or two of Begg Sutherlands' senior managers had come out to India in the indigo days, and had tales to tell of the riotous life of earlier generations of planters; and also, despite all that has been written of their exploitation of the indigo grower in those days, of the parental relationship which the planters had with their own factory hands and farmers. We found evidence of this tradition in the ex-indigo factories, although these were now managed by a new generation of Scottish engineers, chemists and sugar-boilers. Some of them lived in gracious houses set in spacious parks which had been laid out by planter predecessors, landed gentry who had never seen a Clyde-side sugar refinery. Others were less comfortably housed, and for all of them, especially during the crushing season, it was an exacting and lonely life. Yet if I were to suggest some small extravagance at the Corporation's expense, such as a travelling cinema van or a swimming pool, which might relieve in some measure the hardships of our managers, their wives and their empoyees, the proposal would be tested with the unanswerable question, "Aye, but will it put more sugar in the bags?"

Next Elizabeth and I visited the B.I.C.'s woollen mills at Dhariwal, one of the few units outside Uttar Pradesh: it lay just inside India but almost astride the border with Pakistan, in the sensitive area north of Amritsar. The manager of the Dhariwal mills had a problem. In 1947, before the Boundary Commission's award had been made, it had been by no means certain in which country Dhariwal and its mills would find themselves. The manager, sensibly, had two alternative flags ready to hoist on Independence Day. The Pakistan flag was now in his safe: was there any longer a possibility that it might come in useful on a future occasion? What had he better do with it? I told him that it was highly combustible material, and the longer he kept it, the more combustible it would become. He should burn it at dead of night.

Our journeys often took us to Lucknow, political capital of the U.P., fifty miles north of Kanpur. This, in contrast with Kanpur, was an ancient and cultured city, still reflecting some of the atmosphere of the court of the Nawab Vizier and echoes of 'nawabi' days, in the fine speech, food, manners and dandyism of the descendants of the taluqdars of Oudh.

Lucknow was a city of palaces and paper kites. On a suitably breezy day every child in Lucknow seemed to be competing with powdered glass on his kite string, to cut down rival 'birds' which challenged his own from every neighbouring roof-top. Begum Razia Hafazat Hussein, who had lived in Lucknow for many years, a splendidly patrician representative of its elite society, told us a story of political kite-flying.

In 1927 a Statutory Commission headed by Sir John Simon, one of the series of Commissions that toiled to devise equitable conditions for the transfer of power, had arrived in India. They were not welcomed everywhere, and in many places demonstrations of protest were organised. But when they came to Lucknow the loyal and aristocratic Indian hosts were determined that

Kanpur flower show, 1956 (Begum Razia Hussein and Elizabeth)

nothing should mar the entertainment of their guests. On the occasion of a large, formal garden party elaborate precautions were taken to keep the rabble at a distance; but in the middle of the party, and right in the middle of the lawn, an enormous black paper kite plopped down, bearing the inscription 'Simon Go Back!' The hosts had not reckoned with their fellow-citizens' skill at kite-cutting.

The Lucknow portrayed by John Zoffany, and the Lucknow of the free-lance French adventurer, Claude Martin, whose memorial is La Martinere College, has been overlaid by the memory of Mutiny days. The long siege and gallant defence of the Residency, and the bitter fighting on the two occasions of its relief, were vividly recalled by the remains of the building itself, preserved almost as it was on the day when it was finally relieved. There are the battered gateways and bastions, the Redan and the underground chambers built for coolth beneath the Residency itself, which served both as hospital and shelter for families deprived of their homes by the mutineers' bombardment. There also are the cannon of H.M.S. 'Shannon', drawn so far inland to the relief and defence of Lucknow by Peel's naval brigade, who marched with Outram and Havelock from Calcutta. The Union Jack no longer flies over it day and night, but the Residency is maintained as part of India's history and as a battle honour of the Indian army, for loyal Indian troops fought alongside the British and the boys of La Martiniere inside the Residency.

We explored the Ganges near Kanpur, from Bithur twelve miles upstream, where Nana Sahib, of evil memory, adopted son of the last of the Mahratta Peshwas, had lived in exile; past the burning ghats with their gruesome by-products, to a landing-stage below the road-and-rail bridge, shown in the map as Suttee Chowra ghat - but our boatman called it Mansukar ghat, perhaps not connecting the name with massacre. As we stepped ashore we saw a small Hindu temple, inside the railings of which was a simple white stone cross with the inscription: 'In Memoriam - 27th June, 1857'. This was the place where Nana Sahib, having given a promise of safe conduct to Allahabad and provided boats for the 450 men, women and children who survived the siege of Wheeler's entrenchment, ordered his men to set alight the thatched awnings of the boats and kill the occupants as soon as they were aboard, so that only four men escaped, after many adventures, by swimming for their lives. Some of the women and children were made captive, but lived only until, a day before Havelock's relief column reached the city, they too were butchered and thrown into a well.

That well was covered, when I saw it first in 1952, by a masonry plinth, and park-like gardens surrounded it. There had been a marble statue of an angel on the well behind a carved stone screen; but on Independence Day some exuberant youths had chipped the angel's wings, and it had been thought prudent to remove both angel and screen to the comparative privacy of the grounds of the Memorial Church in the cantonments.

A Trust had been set up for the maintenance of the Memorial Gardens. The Indian district magistrate of Kanpur and I were both, at the time I write of, trustees, as successors in office to the original signatories of the Deed. One of the provisions of that Deed was that no masonry structure should ever be built over the site of the well itself.

One evening, walking in the Gardens, I saw unmistakeable signs of new masonry work in progress around and on top of the well. When I got home I telephoned the district magistrate, told him what I had seen and mentioned the terms of the Trust Deed. He was horrified; he was not aware of the Trust, and did not even know where the Memorial Well was. It was understandable; he was a young Rajput, newly arrived in Kanpur, and a massacre is not a page of history which anyone cares to remember. But, what was more embarrassing for him, he had himself recommended to his government that the convenient masonry plinth which he had found in the park near his house, without suspecting its origin, would be an excellent position for a proposed new statue of Tantia Topi.

Tantia Topi was a Mahratta commander who, being a better soldier than most of the mutineers, had given the British a good deal of trouble. He was therefore something of a national hero; but he had been the agent of Nana Sahib in Kanpur at the time of the massacre, and bore a heavy responsibility for it. It was wholly inappropriate that his statue should sit on top of the well.

I sympathised with the district magistrate's predicament, but suggested that, quite apart from his obligations as a trustee, he should consider what kind of impression his plan, if it were proceeded with, would make on public opinion outside India. If the world press should get hold of the story, it would be blown up and distorted and there might be a rumpus, probably the louder the further away it was from Kanpur. I left it to his good sense and feeling to find a way out. I also reported the matter quietly to Malcolm MacDonald, who was the British High Commissioner in Delhi, but asked him to keep it to himself until a solution had been found.

A week later a much relieved district magistrate telephoned me to say he thought he had found the answer. Part of the plan had been, in any case, to make a water garden round the plinth. He now had his government's approval to let that work continue, and to put up Tantia Topi's statue at a discreet distance, say twenty yards, away from the well. I warmly agreed, and congratulated him on this altogether satisfactory outcome. The bare masonry plinth over the well, as it had been left after the angel had been removed, was ugly and untidy. It would now be beautified, and by Indians themselves; while Tantia Topi, at a reasonable distance, would be a penitential ghost, an unobtrusive presence on the scene.

The Memorial Church, to whose garden the angel had been removed, is a large, red brick Victorian gothic building with a capacity for several battalions on church parade. Its echoing emptiness, with the smaller congregation of our time, was not oppressive, but a haven of peace and refreshment, and of comfort in time of trouble. The church had been built on the site of General Sir Hugh Wheeler's entrenchment, the make-shift defences which that veteran commander had prepared in the cantonments, after deciding - a fatal error of judgement - not to risk provoking a local insurrection by moving reliable troops across the city to occupy the more easily defensible Magazine. In that hopeless position the Cawnpore garrison with women and children, about nine hundred in all, of whom less than half were combatants, held out and fought back through the burning days of May and June 1857, without shelter, in open trenches and under continual bombardment, until the approach of the monsoon rains compelled their honourable but doomed capitulation. The gallantry and endurance of such people passes belief.

There was a statue of Queen Victoria in the Mall. One morning early, when not many people were about, I was driving past her and saw some men with a small crane mounted on a lorry, who were trying to wrench the Queen off her pedestal, as if extracting a giant molar. The Superintendent of Police was in charge of the operation. I stopped to observe.

'I'm sorry you have caught us in the act,' said the policeman. 'Orders, you know. We had hoped to finish the job before day-break; but the old lady is tougher than we expected. There is going to be a statue of Gandhiji in her place.'

'What are you going to do with her?'

'Keep her in the police lines, under close arrest, until somebody tells me where to send her.'

In the police lines Queen Victoria stayed for six months, draped in hessian, with her back to the road. I could not see her expression, but I doubt if she was at all amused.

I suggested one day to the Superintendent that he might dispose of Her late Majesty by planting her in the middle of the Ganges. 'Then, every monsoon the river will cover her,' I said, 'and when, in winter, the river level falls, and the crops are ripening, she will emerge from the waters; and before long she will be accepted as the local goddess of fertility.'

He was rather taken with the idea;   but the very next day his orders came to send her to Lucknow;   and there she probably remains to this day, in a damp cellar under the museum, with a number of other effigies of British rule.

In 1957, at a time when I was in some danger of allowing my interests to become completely absorbed in the affairs of the British India Corporation, I was given new horizons by being chosen to be President of the United Kingdom Citizens Association of India.   In the past the President had always been provided by the Calcutta branch of the Association.   The Bombay branch considered it was time that some other branch had a turn, preferably themselves;   and while these two, the largest concentrations of U.K. citizens in India, were settling their difference, they agreed to admit a neutral party, from the Upper India branch of the Association.

It is a healthy tradition among British citizens living abroad that they should organise themselves, as a minority group, for the protection of their own interests, and for the representation of those interests, when necessary, to the government of the host country, without depending, except in emergency, on their own government's Embassy or High Commission.

The presidency of the U.K.C.A. was a rewarding privilege, which kept me in touch with the Government of India and with the British High Commission, as well as with groups of United Kingdom citizens living as far apart as in the Digboi oilfields and tea gardens of Assam, Bombay and the Western seaboard, Bangalore, Madras and the deep south.   A number of interesting problems arose which affected them, ranging from the security of isolated groups, to liquor supplies – imports of whisky had been restricted by the Indian Government to save foreign exchange – and the operation of the British Nationality Act of 1948.

My acquaintance with Pandit Pant, who had left Lucknow to be Home Minister in the Central Government, helped in the matter of security.   I also knew Morarji Desai, then Commerce Minister, in charge of import licensing.   He was a dedicated teetotaller and a stern prohibitionist, and I was not too confident about the reception he would give to a request which I had made, through the proper channels, for a special licence to the U.K.C.A. to import and distribute spirituous liquors to its members.   (It is coincidental that my conversations with authority seemed so often in these days to come round to the subject of spirits).   I had argued that such a concession might reduce the amount of liquor which was smuggled and went straight into the black market.   When I was shown into his office he gave me an acid smile, but I recognised, with relief, that this was for him the equivalent of a broad grin.

'Yes,'he said, 'I know, alas, that whisky is the staff of life for many of your people. But we do not want to drive you away, and shall try not to make life too difficult for you.'

We got the licence.

Many individual problems arose out of the British Nationality Act. I had some myself, and on behalf of my children who had been born in India, of a father also born in India. My own father, who had had the good sense to be born in Singapore, provided the loophole for admitting me - rather grudgingly, I thought - as a citizen of the 'United Kingdom and Colonies', with accent on Colonies. Some years later, when Singapore had ceased to be a colony, I had to provide further justification for my highly suspect birthright, before I could renew my passport. The Act was full of complications and apparent absurdities. The task of legal draftsmen to provide fairly for all cases is a hard one; but, as Maynard Keynes once said, the law is too often concerned with making common-sense illegal. It was galling to find that no obstacles arose for families of African or Chinese origin from Jamaica or Hong Kong, while families of pure British stock who happened to have served abroad for generations, sometimes found it harder to be recognised as citizens of their homeland than to pass through the eye of a needle.

One of our community was a Gladstone, a family who have lived and worked in India for generations. After conning three foolscap pages of the application form for citizenship, none of the questions on which he seemed to be able to answer satisfactorily, he came to the last section, which asked him, in effect, to produce any other reason why his claim should be considered. He wrote in the space provided: 'One of my close relations, was on four occasions Prime Minister of the United Kingdom. I do not know if that counts.'

During my last two and a half years in India I was preoccupied with an extraordinary situation affecting the British India Corporation. I have explained how the Corporation's dividend came to be reduced. After this there had naturally been some decline in the market price of B.I.C. shares, but the decline was modest enough to suggest that the shares were still being bought in some volume. There was nothing surprising in this, as the company's structure was sound and its business profitable. Owing to the system of blank transfers in share dealing which prevailed in India it was not possible to identify any single large purchaser, but it seemed not unlikely, in circumstances which might discourage the small investor, that some powerful Indian interest, possibly Marwari - a race which produces ambitious financiers and industrialists -

was buying up the shares.

At about that time the Government of India decided to review all charitable trusts which were tax-exempt. In the Deed of the MacRobert Trust, which held over thirty percent of B.I.C.'s shares, it was found that one of the objects was 'to perpetuate the ideals of our race and empire', a patriotic sentiment which may have seemed appropriate enough when the Deed was executed, but was not, by any stretch of interpretation, a charitable object, nor one likely to impress the new Indian Government. However, I sought an interview with the Finance Minister in Delhi, and warned him what was likely to happen if the tax exemption of the Trust, our major shareholder, was withdrawn. With a show of remorse the Finance Minister said he wished he could help me; he begged me to take counsel's opinion, but he himself was bound by his advisers, unless the courts upset their conclusion. The tax exemption was withdrawn, with the inevitable consequence. The trustees in London decided that they must sell their large block of B.I.C. shares to the highest acceptable bidder, even though he might not be the most desirable from the Corporation's or even from the national point of view.

The candidate soon came forward; Haridas Mundhra, a Marwari, who made a handsome offer for all of the Trust's shares and for Sir Robert Menzies' own considerable holding, and claimed that he had already acquired enough B.I.C. shares to give him, with these blocks, a clear majority.

Little was known or could be discovered about Mundhra except that he was young, in his thirties, and seemed to have access to a great deal of money – some said the source was Hindu temple funds – and that he had already secured control of several British-managed companies, whose staff he had retained and treated well. Certainly nothing was known against him; he was thought to be a rising star in the Indian financial firmament.

Menzies, who was in England for the summer months when these developments took place, was in favour of the sale of shares to Mundrha going through. Powell, loyal to Begg Sutherlands, wanted to devise means of hiving off that section of the Corporation's interests into surer hands. That course would have taken time, and would have been an open declaration of war on Mundhra, with whom we, the senior management, must try to work, if we were not immediately to desert the Corporation and its staff. I was not so starry-eyed that I did not see possible rocks ahead; but it seemed to me that, in the new India, a combination of British management and British technical skill with Indian financial ability and resources was an experiment worth trying.

So Mundhra acquired the shares and, as soon as Menzies retired in the spring of 1956, became Chairman of the Board. Powell and I remained as managing directors, and I was vice-chairman.

For a few months all went well. Mundhra was full of plans for restoring and enlarging the Corporation; money would be no object. Such plans were welcome to those who knew how much money was needed for the renewal of plant and machinery, and how great the potential of the B.I.C. still was for a useful contribution to the Indian economy.

Mundhra had a keen financial mind, and eye. Although he could write English only with difficulty, and his English vocabulary was limited, he could read a balance sheet upside down, from three feet away, and immediately pick out its salient points. Also he had a certain effusive heartiness, a mannerism not typically Indian, which, for no identifiable reason, made me feel uncomfortable and, fortunately as it turned out, put me on my guard.

Before long proposals and requests for favours and concessions began to reach the management, some directly from Mundhra, others with his recommendation, of a kind which no company Chairman should make without the approval of his Board. The appointment of a friend or a relation to a profitable selling agency; the acquisition of a company, or the sale of stock on delayed payment terms; but mostly for temporary financial accommodation, which did not square with the reports of his personal wealth. At first the proposals were improprieties rather than illegalities, and because of the size and variety of the Corporation's business, Mundhra was sometimes able to slip under our guard, and achieve his object before we were aware of it, by using his authority as Chairman with unsuspecting subordinates. Most of his moves, however, were successfully resisted and, in a series of heart-to-heart talks, I tried to explain what Powell and I understood by 'co-operation' and our prejudice in favour of propriety in the relations of a Chairman with his company. I conceded that there might be a difference of standards, but if he really wanted us to manage the company which he controlled, he must allow us to manage according to our standards. I urged him to apply his own undoubted talents to the good of the Corporation, instead of extracting favours from it.

Whatever Mundhra may have thought about these lectures, he was not yet prepared for an open breach. He thanked me for my frankness and said he would try to understand my point of view. He admitted that before he had had anything to do with the B.I.C, he had committed some peccadilloes which were an embarrassment to him. But now he had turned over a new leaf –

or rather, he intended to do so at any moment, as soon as he had put right just one or two outstanding matters. It was for this that he sometimes found himself in need of a little help, to square his accounts at the end of the month – but he would certainly bear in mind all that I had said. Then, if I was not quick enough to evade his grasp, he would put his arm round my shoulder and try to clasp me to his ample bosom, exclaiming that he felt towards me as a son towards his father, that I brought out all his better instincts, that I made him feel good.

I was not so much reassured as alarmed. I felt that I might at any moment be called upon to take the place of the Brahmin priest, the personal chaplain that Mundhra carried around with him everywhere as a spiritual adviser.

But the position was rapidly becoming an impossible one, for Mundhra as well as ourselves. By various channels the news began to reach us that Mundhra had decided to get rid of Powell and myself – we were too 'orthodox', we were obstinate, we were not 'co-operative'. I too decided that the experiment had failed and that I could not work with Mundhra; but I could not desert the Corporation before Powell and I had put it, so far as possible, in a state of defence. The process took time: it was not a rearguard action so much as a holding action while we looked for allies and tried to secure the position of the staff. In all that we did, although we risked misunderstanding by inability to explain or communicate all our plans and actions, we had the trust and loyal support of most – unfortunately not of all – our British and Indian colleagues in the B.I.C. management and on the Board.

I was in the unhappy position that I could not myself be loyal to the Corporation and, at the same time, to such a chairman as Haridas Mundhra. I warned our bankers of the way things were going, for they provided a large seasonal overdraft, mainly for buying wool, cotton, hides and sugar cane, and I wished to enlist their help in avoiding the effects of a sudden collapse of confidence. I also warned the Government of India who had an interest in the B.I.C.'s welfare, because of the large contracts they placed for army clothing and boots. It was a calculated risk of precipitating a panic intervention which would have done more damage than it cured; but both Bank and Government respected my confidence and, in the event, proved to be powerful, if rather slow and clumsy allies.

The story of the eighteen months' struggle to keep our Chairman on the rails and to protect the B.I.C from his designs would be tedious. Suspicion itself can become a tedious obsession, and I had to suspect every move and statement that Mundhra made, although we still had to work together. The managements of his other companies, in Calcutta and Bombay, were having much the same experience, but with less success. Mundhra knew, I think, that I kept a log of all our meetings and discussions, bewildering in their variety and frequency, so that towards the end there were almost hourly entries. I took care to have these confirmed by the signatures of others who may have taken part, but there were not always witnesses. Although Mundhra tried increasingly to bypass me in getting what he wanted, there was not much he could achieve without discussing it with me, which meant an entry in the log. I believe that this deterred him from committing a criminal act so far as the B.I.C. was concerned, until, in the autumn of 1957, he became desperate.

The climax came one day when Mundhra entered my office bringing a seemingly straight-forward offer from a 'friend' to buy a large quantity of cloth from one of our mills, where, as he knew, stocks had accumulated to an embarrassing extent. Payment would be made, he proposed, at the market price, but since the amount was large, only half of the price would be paid cash down. The other half would be paid after six months, with security for the deferred payment. He laid the security on my desk, a bundle of share certificates of one of his other companies, with blank transfer deeds signed by the manager of a Calcutta bank and stamped with its seal.

I said that, as a formality, I would have to verify the transfer from the bank. Mundhra did not flicker an eyelid. 'Very well,' he said, 'but please address your enquiry not to the bank but to the bank manager personally.' He must have had his reasons for this.

I sent to the manager of the Calcutta bank a list of numbers of the share certificates for verification. Nothing happened for several days. Meanwhile I discovered that part of the cloth to be supplied on credit had already been removed from the mill, on Mundhra's instructions, which I immediately countermanded. I sent a reminder to the bank, this time not to the manager by name, and had a reply by telegram to say that the earlier letter had not been received. I repeated this letter, this time enclosing one of the transfer deeds. The reply came immediately, saying that the bank still held certificates with the serial numbers I had quoted, and that the signature on the transfer deed and the bank's seal were both forgeries.

Mundhra was in my room a few minutes after I had opened this letter.

'You have had a letter from the bank' he said. He did not ask me what was in it. 'What are you going to do?'

'I have to consider,' I said. 'You have put me in a very difficult position.'

'If you are not satisfied with the security, let me replace

those share certificates with others.'
That would have been fatal.

'No, Haridas. It may be that you will now have to do your
paraschit' - a Sanskrit religious term meaning atonement. That
was the only time that I ever saw Mundhra wince.

The next day I had to go to Calcutta on business. I could
not leave the share certificates in the B.I.C. strongroom, with
Mundhra in Kanpur while I was away. So that night a
conspiratorial party consisting of Elizabeth and myself,
embarked on a cloak-and-dagger mission. Our house, I knew, was
watched and our movements reported to Mundhra. I suspected also
that our telephone line and even our conversation in the house
were not free from eavesdroppers. We should therefore have to
go about our business deceptively, and with as few words as
possible. Keys of the strongroom were held by the Treasurer, a
European; but the Assistant Treasurer, a Bengali, had a
duplicate set. I had reason to doubt the discretion of the
Treasurer, and in any case did not wish to explain my plan to
him. The Assistant would do what I required without asking
questions.

We drove out as if we were going to the Club; then by a
circuitous route to the Bengali's house, and luckily found him
at home. I told him to come along with me, bringing his keys.
At Sutherland House, the Corporation's office building, the
night guard let us in, with much saluting and stamping of boots
to emphasise his wakefulness. Occasional office crises which
turned night into day did not surprise him, and he wanted to
flood the building in a blaze of light to mark the Managing
Director's visit. I said one light inside the building would be
enough, as we were not staying long. In the strongroom itself
we used hand torches. We quickly found the bundle of share
certificates and transfer deeds; I gave the Assistant Treasurer
a receipt for them, and took them back to Elizabeth waiting in
the car.

We returned to our own house, had a drink and let the
servants go to bed. Then we took the bundle to an inner room
and made a large sealed package of it.

It was now nearly mid-night. If the house was being
watched, our next excursion might have attracted attention; but
it was a short journey, to the house of the Indian manager of
the local branch of the State Bank of India. We parked the car
under some trees in the dark compound, where both the gate and
the house entrance could be seen. Elizabeth, who had heard
rumours about designs on my person, was determined to accompany
me as far as possible as a bodyguard; and this time she bravely
volunteered to stay in the car alone, to see if we had been

followed, for it was important that Mundhra should not know where I had lodged the certificates. Meanwhile I roused Mr. Krishnan, the manager, who had gone to bed; fortunately he and I were old friends. I apologised for the eccentric hour of my call, but assured him there was good reason for it. I asked him to keep the package in safe custody, in my own name. Did he want to know what was in it? He shook his head.

Before I left for Calcutta on the next morning I reported to the district magistrate what I had done, promised an explanation later and asked him to await events. I saw Mundhra's spies at the railway station, waiting to see in which direction I would go. Mundhra expected me, I think, to go straight to report to the authorities in Delhi, and was no doubt relieved to hear that I had caught the Calcutta Mail, for he knew that I had a previously arranged engagement there. If I was still considering my course of action it would give him some time to arrange - I know not what. Perhaps he hoped to recover the certificates somehow, or even to organise an unfortunate accident, to the certificates or to myself.

In Calcutta I went immediately to my friend, Sachin Chaudhuri, an eminent lawyer and a director of the State Bank, who was later to be Finance Minister in India. He heard my story and whistled. He said I had taken on a packet of trouble, but told me to leave it to him; and then he let me out of his office by the side door. In due course the processes of law began to move.

Haridas Mundhra's _paraschit_ was a long sentence for cheating and forgery. In the course of his trial he exhausted two counsel in his defence, and he nearly exhausted me, for I spent about thirty hours in the witness boxes of various courts, being the principal, almost the only material witness. The ramifications of the case were complicated, and I was glad that I had kept my hourly log-book. Haridas would sometimes put in an appearance himself in court, but, in spite of being the accused in a criminal case, he had usually managed to obtain permission to be elsewhere. When he came he would interrupt the proceedings by greeting me loudly and waving cheerfully from the back of the court to me in the witness box, as if we were old friends and nothing had come between us. I had certainly come to know him pretty well.

The strange thing about this not wholly unlikeable rogue is that, although completely amoral in business - perhaps supralegal is a better word - he appeared to be a devout and religious man, so far as Hindu observance went. He was not a Brahmin, but claimed superiority in caste to some of his fellow Marwaris in Kanpur - to Sir Padampat Singhania, for instance; and he once admitted to me that he found it convenient to have a

good excuse for not dining with Sir Padampat. He only stayed
once in our house, and then special arrangements had to be made
for his drinking water for, as he apologetically explained to
me, he had examined the mechanism of the pump in the well which
supplied our water, and discovered that it had leather washers.
Water which had come in contact with cow-hide would defile his
lips. He would not have endangered his prospects of promotion
in a reincarnated state by omitting his morning bathe in the
Ganges; and for extra precaution he made his cook have a dip
too, before he prepared any meal for him. By these
superstitious gestures, of course, he obtained absolution for
minor or involuntary sins. But crimes like cheating and forgery
were not sinful in his eyes: they were merely breaches of a
man-made law, itself no more than a collection of obstacles
designed for the enterprising to circumvent, taking a gambler's
chance in pursuit of his objective, which, in his own case, was
material prosperity in an unreal world. Out of the proceeds, if
his luck held, he would probably build temples or endow
hospitals - as others of his community had done.

In different circumstances Mundhra might have been a Hindu
ascetic, equally contemptuous of the obligations and the
illusions of the world. Simple, orthodox people like Christie
and Powell, who were neither serious gamblers nor ascetics,
could not help blurring the obvious distinction between sin and
crime. Whatever the courts might say, it was not he but
'Christies-and-Powells' who were in error. Towards the end he
had magnified us into a composite, plural monster who stood in
the way of his material and spiritual fulfilment.

The purchase of the B.I.C. shares had overstretched
Mundhra's 'resources'. The criminal prosecution gave rise to an
enquiry from which it transpired that he had been duplicating,
nay multiplying share certificates of various companies which he
controlled, and using the worthless paper as security for large
overdrafts with a number of banks, and for other loans and
advances. He would move the deposits round, not leaving them
long enough in one place for the fraud to be detected - so long
as there was no reason to suspect his good faith. That was the
secret of his wealth. It was a simple confidence trick, which
has been practised by others; a gamble on the element of trust
which there must be initially between the parties to most
business transactions. It can succeed, for a time, and succeed
spectacularly if it is done on a large enough scale. But it can
also corrupt and destroy, both companies and people. India had
to get men like Haridas Mundhra out of her system.

While the case was going on the State Bank of India
foreclosed on the B.I.C.'s overdraft and put in a Receiver, as a
protective measure, although the Corporation was far from being

insolvent. It was done with the best intentions, but it caused almost as many complications as Mundhra had done. Ronald Powell and I stayed on for a time as the Receiver's assistants. Later, the Government of India, under special powers, replaced the Receiver with a nominated Board. The B.I.C.'s shares recovered, and now the Corporation is back in the hands of its shareholders and a properly elected Board.

Cawnpore was now at last and truly Kanpur. The transfer of power in India had not been easy or bloodless, but it had been dignified by some historical significance. The transfer of industrial power on the smaller stage of Kanpur had been a less edifying experience. It was unpleasant while it lasted, but the British India Corporation was saved.

Now it was time for our drums to beat Retreat.

In February 1959 Elizabeth and I said goodbye to Kanpur and to India, where I had served in various capacities for more than thirty years. For me India was not a land of regrets, and, although I did not know it then, she had not seen the last of me.

We boarded a P & O ship in Bombay, with emotions on my part, more mature and more thankful than those which had inspired me to verse in the 'Rawalpindi' so many years ago. I did not throw my topi over the stern: I had no topi to throw. It was the symbol of a vanished age.

Soon it was good to see the coastline of Europe once more, the flush of almond blossom around the toe of Italy, and the mimosa in bloom along the Riviera.